Also by Paul Duffau

Finishing Kick, a novel

A Walk with Rose
(a short story)

Trail of
Second
Chances

PAUL DUFFAU

Trail of Second Chances

Published 2014 by Cruiser Publications
www.cruiserpublications.com

Cover art by Kit Foster
www.kitfosterdesign.com

Book design copyright © 2014
Cruiser Publications

ISBN 13- 978-0-9889479-3-1

Trail of
Second
Chances

For Katie, Lyn, and Sara

Chapter 1

Becca felt sweat roll down her temples as the plastic mask strapped to her face threatened to suffocate her and the metallic-tasting air made her want to gag.

"Don't quit," Rob, her father, said in a quiet voice beside her.

She gave him a withering look and continued to pound away on the treadmill.

Past him sat sixty-three runners attending the Bitterroot Running Clinic, most of them staring at her. The coaches had set up the area and arranged the runners in a semicircle around the apparatus. When she had stepped forward—involuntarily— to be the guinea pig, there had been murmuring as the attendees compared notes. She'd stood on the treadmill, donned the mask, and the torture had begun.

The plastic mask was attached to tubing, sending the used air to an analyzer that would beep once when she reached the point where she couldn't use any more air, when the lactic acid in her system built up faster than the circulatory system could cleanse it.

When I hit exhaustion, she thought. The thought triggered another bout of claustrophobia and the mask pressed tighter to her cheeks.

Technically, the test measured for oxygen uptake—how much air she could process while she ran. Runners shortened it to VO_2 *max*, and it was one of the holy grails of runner performance. Form could be taught and tactics could be learned but only the fairy godmother of genetics could tap you with the magic wand that sent you to the Olympics. One tap, and an ungodly amount of hard work.

"Keep digging, Becca, you can do this."

On the other side of the treadmill, monitoring the equipment, was Jim Eagle, cross-country coach at Bridger College in Missoula.

"You're doing great, Becca. Just hang in a little longer," said Eagle, his dark eyes scanning the instruments. A former Olympian in the five thousand meters, the coach was a small, intense man and a full-blooded Nez Perce Indian. He was an alternate when the man ahead of him, a young hotshot from UCLA, blew out both an Achilles tendon and his running career at the same time in a pickup basketball game.

The incline on the treadmill went up incrementally and Becca struggled to keep up. Gulping air, she tucked her chin down as her thighs started to burn. The display of the treadmill was blurry and she wiped a wet arm across her eyes to clear them but all she accomplished was getting more saltiness into her eyes. They burned and her quads were worse, on fire. The acid was building. This was the third time she had been tested— her father volunteered her every year that she came to camp— and she knew that it was almost over but kept fighting to push the point of failure as far from her as she could.

This is the way the stupid mouse feels, she thought, a picture of a small white rodent chasing through a maze while people in white lab coats took notes. She stumbled slightly from loss of concentration. Sweat came off in rivulets, and plastered her shirt to her back. She felt the wobble in her shoulders and tried to hide it.

"Keep going," said Rob Hawthorne just as the machine signaled the end of the test. The deck of the treadmill began to drop as the belt slowed. Becca slowed with it.

"Can I take off the mask?" she asked, panting, voice muffled by the plastic. She looked at Eagle, eyes pleading.

"Sure, go ahead," he replied.

She reached behind her head and struggled to get the elastic bands at the back loosened while she kept running, dropping pace to match the slowing belt. The mask clung to her sweaty face before detaching with a sucking pull. Becca, her lungs already in recovery, dragged in a great, gasping breath.

The treadmill slowed to a stop and Becca stepped off, legs unsteady on the motionless floor. Her dad handed her a water bottle and she took several gulps, the icy water sending a refreshing chill down her throat. As she was reaching for a towel to wipe off with, Eagle threw the data from her test up onto a large-screen monitor.

Her eyes, along with those of the other runners, tracked to the screen, where three lines were traced, blue for oxygen, red for carbon monoxide, and yellow for heart rate. Where the red and blue crossed is where it hurt.

"You've improved," murmured Rob, analyzing the graph. "But you still have some room to grow." He glanced at her. "Good job."

Ignoring him, she threw her towel in the corner and went to sit with the other campers.

Eagle left the testing equipment and stood by the monitor.

"Okay, here is how this works." Quickly he explained the lines and what the axes represented—oxygen consumption on one axis, time on the other.

"As you can see, Becca was running easily and had no trouble getting enough air in early—see the gap?" he asked, pointing to the chart at the five-minute mark. "But when we got to the end of the test, that gap narrowed until the lines crossed."

Eagle looked over the group. "Uptake isn't the only factor we look at in running, and some of you are probably very accomplished runners even without high uptakes. Running economy—how efficient you are—makes a huge difference.

"Becca has both. Her scores here, a 68.7 VO_2 max, is superior, especially for a high school athlete. Elite, well-trained females can get to about 75, guys can get to about 85, though scores over 90 have been recorded."

He thumbed the clicker in his hand and the screen revealed another chart. Becca recognized it and saw the point where the panic attack had almost caused her to fall on the treadmill her freshman year.

"This is Becca two years ago. As you can see, she's improved a great deal. That's the good news. You can improve uptake. The bad news is that you can only improve it this much," he said, holding his hands apart about a foot. "That's why we're focusing on form this year. The base miles and speed work are great and you need those, but most of you get it in your programs already."

He nodded to Becca's dad. "The goal this year is to help you make those miles and the speed more effective by helping you become more efficient. Coach Hawthorne, for those that don't know him, is one of the top high school coaches in Montana, and an expert at developing form. A lot of the drills we're going to teach you we use here and are adapted from his program."

Heads turned to Becca's dad but she kept her eyes on Jim Eagle. Her dad was an expert. She knew that, had listened to his instructions to drop her arms, tuck her elbows, increase her back kick until she was ready to puke.

Eagle smiled. "And I promise this is the last really nerdy thing we're going to do here. Those of you who have been to the Bitterroot Running Clinic know the routine. We'll have an easy run in the morning, followed by breakfast and a lecture. After-noons are play time—we have the river right there so we can go tubing or swimming—or you can take a nap. We'll do an evening run, a short one before dinner. That one is optional. Nights we relax and play some games."

The athletes, a mix of teenage boys and girls, were getting restless. Eagle recognized the signs. His runners, some of them, were only a year or two older than Becca.

"Okay, enough," he said. "Time to load up. Let's head for the mountains."

Runners scrambled to their feet, eager to be moving again.

Her dad intercepted her as she walked toward the vans that would ferry them to the cabins.

"You did a good job in there," he said. He reached for one of her bags. "Want some help?"

"I got it."

He withdrew the offending hand and started to walk with her. "This is a good opportunity for you."

Becca turned her head to watch the first of the kids loading their sleeping bags and clothes into the back of the van, squash-ing the bags to make room.

"Becca."

She stopped because he did, and turned to face him.

"What, Dad? What's a great opportunity?"

Annoyance lit his eyes briefly before it disappeared with the smallest of head shakes. His tone had a slightly reproving tone when he said, "You're an upperclassman now. You have a chance to show the younger kids"—he indicated them with his head, the gangly freshmen with the pinched, scared look—"what it takes to be a runner. A lot of these kids, the girls at least, look up to you."

She looked them over and then returned her gaze to her dad, but staring at his shoulder, not his eyes.

"They shouldn't."

A sigh. "But they will and you can't change that. It comes with the territory. There's not a girl over there that doesn't wish she could run like you. Probably," he said, but not boasting, "none of them ever will. They'll never win State, they'll never go to the Foot Locker Championships except as a spectator." He waited while his words sank in.

"So what am I supposed to do, *Coach* Hawthorne?" She regretted it as soon as she said it. At practice, he was Coach, but the rest of the time he was just Dad.

"For starters, you might try acting like you want to be here," he said, annoyance creeping into his voice.

Becca felt her lips tighten and her body get rigid. *It's you I don't want here,* she thought, but she said, "I like the clinic just fine. And I like the kids mostly."

She could feel her dad staring at her and she sneaked a glance at his face. The anger was gone, replaced by resignation.

"Okay," he said, in a subdued voice, "I understand." He chose his words carefully. "You only get one shot at this, right now. There aren't any do-overs and you don't always get a second chance."

Becca shot an angry glance at him.

"Know when," he said, the intensity of his stare making her shift uncomfortably, "to go for it, to seize the opportunity."

"Can you still keep up with her?"

Rob, watching Becca rejoin the group, switched his attention to the petite woman who had joined him.

"Barely." He smiled ruefully and said, "When she turns it all the way up, it pretty well kills me, especially the last year or so."

"Doesn't surprise me," said Sandi, Jim's wife. "She's grown just since the last time you guys came out for a visit." She gave him an appraising look. "She's not a little girl anymore."

Rob winced and turned to walk back to the gym the kids had just left. Sandi turned with him and put a hand on his arm, bringing him to a halt. Bemused, he stopped to look at her.

"What?"

"Would you stop worrying?" she asked.

"I'm a dad," he said. "It comes with the territory."

"Most dads are worried about boys at this age."

"Becca hasn't shown a whole lot of interest—"

"Yet," Sandi said in mock seriousness.

"Thanks, that makes me feel so much better."

Sandi chuckled, a vivacious sound that floated on the breeze, and they started to walk again. "She looked frustrated."

Rob let out a low, disgruntled sigh and said, "She's in a hurry."

"Can you blame her? She's sixteen; they're all in a hurry in one way or another. She's just set herself a really high bar."

Rob shrugged. "It's too early to know for sure, but if she keeps developing—and doesn't blow herself up," he added, "she has as good a shot as anybody."

"Except most of those girls don't have Dad as coach, and, as good as she is, she might still not be the best in her own family," said Sandi, reaching out to touch Rob's arm again. "I'm not criticizing. It's tough for both of you."

Rob gave her a wry grin. "Yeah, but that's what she wants. Or says she does."

"Are you sure that's all she wants?" asked Sandi.

Seeing the tension the comment created in Rob, Sandi changed subjects. "I love to watch her run. She paused. "She just floats, like you used to."

Rob shook his head, blocking out the thought.

Jim Eagle barged out the doors, toting a couple of boxes of paperwork. "We got to hustle," he said as he took fast strides toward his waiting vehicle.

"I'm going to run my own rig up to the camp," said Rob, grabbing the door before it fully closed. "You need me to throw anything else in the back?" Rob drove a Suburban, a big reliable vehicle for hauling cross-country kids to meets.

"Think we're good," Jim said over his shoulder. "Let's go, the vans are ready to roll."

"He'll think of fourteen things we forgot before we leave the highway," said Sandi, turning toward the parking lot. "What does Angela think?"

He ran a hand through his sandy blond hair as he walked next to her, considering her question. "She thinks I'm pushing too hard," he said. The sliver of a rueful smile that showed on his face when he talked of his wife was quickly replaced by frustration. "And Becca thinks I'm going too slow." He paused to let out a long breath. "And she's right. But Jim and I can both recall great early runners who did too much, too soon, and ended up broken."

"Like maybe her dad?" asked Sandi, a touch of sadness in the subtle inflections of her words.

"It's not the same," Rob said, "and life happens—at least, if everything goes right." He flicked his eyes at her. "Besides, it was worth it."

They stepped up the pace as the first of the vans fired up the engine and eased away from the curb. Rob angled toward his vehicle.

"Rob?"

He stopped and half turned.

"Give her a little room and a chance. She'll get there."

Rob nodded but said, "A chance is what I need Becca to take. She plays it too safe. Sometimes you got to follow your gut and just launch."

Sandi's eyes reflected a quiet sadness.

"Just humor her godmother, would you? . . . Give her a little time to finish growing up?"

Becca leaned her head against the warm glass and felt the vibration of the engine, quick and steady, lulling her. Her father was right. The young runners, the girls, had all treated her like she was different and wouldn't even look at her as they asked questions, half afraid that she would do . . . *what*?

That first Foot Locker, when she was a freshman and still scared, she had finished in a disappointing—to her and, she supposed, to her dad—twenty-first place. She remembered the look in the eyes of the girls—the nationally recognized racers, the ones that got written up in the running magazines. They all had the same look. She wondered if they shared the same feeling.

All I want to do is run. . . .

Chapter 2

The room was primitive—rough-hewn lumber for the walls and floors, an open window to let the flies in, and zero privacy separating the four bunks—and Becca was relieved to be there.

She threw her stuff on the top bunk on the east side of the cabin. The advantage of arriving first, she thought.

"Rebecca," said a familiar voice behind her, accenting the first syllable of her name and softening it to *Rah-becca*.

With a smile that lit a happy glow in her eyes, she whirled and ran to the slender young man at the door, giving him a hug. *"Jambo,"* she said in his native tongue, stepping back from the friendly embrace.

"You remember," Joseph Obado said with a laugh. "It is good to see you."

"Of course," she said.

Joseph had lived with her family for a year when he moved to America from Kenya. Becca's dad, on one of his frequent trips to the country, had "discovered" Joseph in a remote village, and had marveled at the speed that Joseph displayed running for class, late because of his chores. With a promise to the teenage boy's family that Joseph would be treated like his own son, her dad had persuaded Joseph to leave his country for the strangeness of Montana. He was part of the wave of incredible runners from Africa that flooded every distance event, from the eight hundred meters to the marathon.

"What are you doing here? Dad said you were headed east after graduation."

Joseph smiled, a broad white flash in his dark face. "Not yet. First I went home to see my family." A small cloud of concern passed through his eyes.

"Hard?"

Joseph's voice was soft and his eyes were distant. "I have been very comfortable here. I forgot how hard everybody there must work just to eat." He laughed again and he focused his gaze on Becca. "And I'm not going East, I'm going to Chicago, which is in the Midwest."

"Is it a good job?"

"It is a good position and the firm is very reputable, but I believe that they want me more as a runner than an economist." He shrugged. "They will get both, and I will attend the University of Chicago for my master's. Everybody will be happy." Again the cloud crossed and passed.

A taller, dark-haired girl appeared in the doorway and surveyed the cabin, an eyebrow arching as she took in the details.

"Kind of a dump," she said. She hefted her gear and sleeping bag while she decided which of the remaining bunks to take.

"Rebecca, I should be helping Coach Eagle," said Joseph, shooting a fast glance to the new arrival. "I will see you at the afternoon meeting."

"Sure thing," she said to Joseph's tapered back as the young man left. She turned to the girl. "The bottom bunk over here will be the coolest in the evening when you're trying to sleep."

The girl eyed the bunk, switched her gaze to Becca's gear on the top bunk, and nodded. "Thanks." She walked over and dumped her possessions onto the lower bunk. She turned around to face Becca again. "I'm Dana."

"Becca."

The two girls stood still, sizing each other up. The new girl was taller and bigger than Becca but still had that same lean look and her black hair was tied up in a ponytail. The dark eyes appraising Becca were steady, and while Becca was pretty sure that she was older, there was something *mature* about the look Dana was giving her. She knew what the other girl saw—a lithe girl who looked perpetually thirteen. Becca was a late bloomer, which didn't help on the race course against the older, more developed girls. It frustrated the hell out of her every time they beat her with muscle and kicks; she fought them with guts, guile, and a stride built to cover ground fast.

"First time at this camp?"

"Yeah. You've been here before." Dana made it a statement rather than a question. The Bitterroot Clinic attracted runners from the Pacific Northwest, even pulling in some from as far away as Alaska. Some campers returned every year but most looked for different camps and clinics each year, honing a new skill or searching for the one secret tip that would put them at the top of the podium.

Becca shrugged. "Plenty. I got to come before high school because my dad is one of the coaches."

"You come every year then." Again a statement.

"Whether I want to or not."

Dana nodded. "I went to Oregon last year. It's nice to mix it up."

Becca scrutinized Dana's face and it dawned on her that she had seen the girl before at a race, last year. Becca had beaten Dana—she memorized the faces of the three girls that she hadn't beat and planned to get even this year—but she recognized Dana because she was a freshman. A freshman who had managed to stay close for more than half of the race. Someone to keep track of, to avoid getting surprised.

"You're Rodriguez. You were at the regionals."

Dana shrugged. "I'm surprised you remember. You and the others pretty well tore it up there in front."

Becca did not respond. As a freshman—she didn't look it, thought Becca a bit enviously—Dana was considered one of the next great runners coming out of the Northwest.

Dana interrupted her mingled thoughts and memories.

"So what now?"

"We wait. We'll have at least one, maybe two girls show up looking for a bunk." Becca smiled. "The newbies always head to the cabins by the river, but there's no trees."

Dana looked confused and Becca looked at her in surprise. "You didn't notice?"

Dana shook her head. "I saw you headed this way and figured you knew the best spots, so I followed you."

"The cabins by the river get super hot in the afternoon—nothing to block the sun. At night, it's like trying to sleep in a sauna." She nodded to their bunks. "Our bunks will be the first to cool down and the breeze comes right through the window," she lazily pointed with her right hand, "and we can still hear the river."

"You thought of all this?"

"I learned it—my first year, I was right there at the river and cooked. I must have lost five pounds in sweat every night before it cooled down."

Dana's eyes slid up and down Becca. "You don't have five pounds to lose. You're already tiny."

Becca laughed. "Look who's talking. You ever read Jim Fixx's book? I forget the title now but he said if you got enough runners together, you had a 'convention of cadavers.' "

Dana's nose wrinkled at the mention of a book but then her eyes crinkled in the corners with humor. "We're fast cadavers."

Becca laughed again.

Two more girls, sisters, showed up about ten minutes later and grabbed the remaining two bunks. Everybody introduced themselves, a swarm of noise and hellos, before getting their gear stowed out of the way. Basic housekeeping accomplished, the foursome headed for the lodge, where the vans were parked. On the way, they met one of the camp counselors, Sara, a runner in Eagle's program. She checked to make sure the girls were settled in.

"Okay, right," said the counselor. "Becca, you headed to the lodge?" Seeing Becca bobbing her head in the affirmative, she continued, "Okay, ladies. Snacks inside, and the first seminar is in about an hour." The girl, only a few years older than them, sped off to round up the next group of runners. Across the camp, other counselors, most of them runners in local college programs, did the same.

The interior of the lodge was dim and Becca paused in the entrance for the second it took for her eyes to adjust. Off to the right, she saw the snack table set up, while to the left, benches were set into rows. She went right and filled her water bottle.

"Don't forget to drink," she reminded the others. "We're high enough that we can get dehydrated real quick." The camp sat in a high valley in the Bitterroot Mountains dividing Montana and Idaho, with the taller peaks scraping the skies. Trapper Peak, faintly visible in the distance, was still snow covered. She grabbed a handful of nuts and an apple from the table. On the far wall, she spied a trail map of the wilderness area surrounding their temporary home.

She meandered over to it and located the camp—the bright red star helped—on the topographical maps. There were three on the wall. The star sat in a broad green expanse indicating the valley. White areas bordered the green where the peaks of the mountains sat to the west. The contour lines, spidery black squiggles that showed elevation changes, bunched tightly at the peaks, representing the precipitous cliffs and rocky passages to the top.

"What are you looking at?" asked Dana. She peered at the map, trying to make sense of the markings.

"It's a topo of the area," Becca explained. When Dana looked lost, she explained. "Topo maps show you the elevation changes, mountains, lakes, rivers, stuff like that. See," she said, "we're here." Her finger tapped on the star. "This blue line is the river. The green shows forest; white, clearings." Quickly, she ran down the meaning of the contour lines and pointed out the trails and roads.

"Confusing," admitted Dana.

"It's not too bad once you get used to it."

Dana continued to look doubtful and wandered away. More runners came in under the watchful eyes of the staff and the room got noisy as kids swapped names and made awkward conversation while they waited for the first speaker. A few kids, the real loners, stood around the outside walls watching the others but making no attempt to socialize. One by one, they were picked off by the staff, who gently eased them into the mob in the middle of the room, introducing them to the older campers.

Becca took it all in at a glance. The pattern repeated every year and she had learned to fake interest in something—anything—to avoid the counselors. She turned back to the map. Off to one side, near the camp but on the other side of the West Fork River, a new trail, sketched in red ink, dropped from the main trail system down to the river east of them. Impulsively, she reached out and traced the route with a finger, following it to the tributary where it turned and followed another river. Farther on, it reached a bridge and then a forest road.

"It's an old trail that my people used during our seasonal migrations," said Jim Eagle, his voice at her side startling her. He reached past her to retrace the route, explaining as he went.

"We followed food in the days when we still owned our land." His finger tapped at the top of the trail. "This was a longer route, but easier for women and children to climb to this lake"—another tap on the map, this time well past the point where the trails connected—"in the summer. The men hunted and fished, and the women gathered roots and berries. Before winter, they climbed down the same way to get to the lower meadows and the camps along the rivers. They followed this trail"—his finger was now parallel to the river—"to the confluence."

Becca absorbed the information and then asked, "So why is it in red?"

Eagle looked at the map and a faraway look came into his eyes. "The mapmakers from the Geological Service ignored it, seeing only the steeper hunting trail." He looked at Becca. "One of our very old women remembered traveling it. It took me days to find it. I started clearing the trail last year."

She glanced away from the topo to look at him. "I thought that was Forest Service land. You're not allowed to just tear things up, right? I mean, I've helped on trails, digging out rock and cutting brush," she said, referring to volunteer work she had done the previous summer. "They let you have a permit?"

Eagle's eyes went very dark. "I didn't ask."

Becca felt a chill and stared at the coach.

The look faded and he continued. "It was our land first." He laughed. "I'll get a lawyer and that's what we'll argue. The Feds hate to fight the Tribe, and it isn't hurting anything." He laughed again and said, "You've gotten very good at hiding in plain sight. Come on, join the rest of the group. The first seminar is about to start anyway."

Becca's head jerked around. "Hiding?"

"You thought nobody noticed?" He indicated the front of the room where Joseph was setting up the lectern for the speaker. "I have my sources."

Joseph looked up as though he could feel the pressure of her glare, and he smiled. When she scrunched her face into a mock-angry look, the smile got wider. He gave a gentle shake of his head and went back to work, stringing the wiring.

She allowed Eagle to lead her toward the other runners. As she walked, her eyes kept moving, and she saw her father walk in, looking agitated. He scanned the room before settling on Joseph. He strode briskly across the room, dodging the kids with deft sidesteps. He launched into conversation before he got to Joseph, but his words were too low to be heard. Joseph's initial smile faded into sadness and he bobbed his head once, slowly, and shrugged his narrow shoulders. Rob Hawthorne spoke again, and turned from the young Kenyan.

Becca's eyes narrowed, her curiosity piqued, and she slipped past Eagle, walking toward Joseph. Her father, following her with his eyes, changed course to intercept her. He stepped in front of her and blocked her path.

"Leave it, Becca-bear," he said as the anger in his eyes bled into his voice.

She looked over his shoulder and said, "What's going on?"

"Nothing for you to worry about." His voice was tight and controlled. "I may miss this evening's session. I have to make a speed run to Missoula. I'll be back as quick as I can."

"Why? What's it got to do with Joseph?"

"Nothing for you to worry about," he said, "and you leave Joseph alone. He doesn't need you bothering him right now." He shook his head. "I'll be back soon." He spun abruptly and, with quick strides, walked to the door. When he was three steps from Becca, he turned and spoke again.

"The slots on the mountain run are full. I signed you up for the last spot."

Volunteered again, she thought as her father stalked toward the doorway. Angry and defiant, she turned to look for Joseph anyway, but he was gone.

Chapter 3

The morning run started during a vivid dawn that splashed soft hues across the sky. As the runners eased out, a lone cloud reflected the colors down to them, brightening with the emerging sun until it glowed golden at the edges. By the time they returned, the colorful cloud was washing out in the bright, already hot sun.

Becca jogged to a stop, barely breathing hard. They covered about three miles, and she had run with the girls instead of the faster boys so she could save her legs for the mountain trail run in the afternoon. She had tried to transfer to the group led by Coach Eagle but her father had rebuffed her efforts, keeping her in his group.

Dana, standing next to her, said, "Time to eat." She stretched the way a big cat would, a long, languid motion that started at her toes and rippled up to her fingertips extended above her head. A small crack from her back sounded as tension released from the joints. "That feels better."

Becca's nostrils flared as the smell of bacon drifted in the slight breeze. She wasn't the only one—around her, the girls shifted, glanced around, and, in ones and twos, turned and walked to the dining hall.

Becca nudged Dana with an elbow. "Come on." Dana followed Becca toward breakfast.

After the bright sunlight, the interior of the dining hall was dim and still cool from the night air and the shade of the evergreens. By dinnertime, the room would be a hot box. Becca and Dana grabbed silverware and trays from the stack and joined the back of the line.

Behind the warming tables, staff hurried, swapping out pans as quickly as the girls emptied them. The staff alternated duty, one group up early one day to do the cooking, the next day to run with the kids, shepherding them out into the dawn while the other team of counselors worked up breakfast.

"Eat up, ladies, we got plenty," said a blond-haired young man as he dropped a steaming pan of fried potatoes into an open slot in the table. Becca loaded her plate with potatoes and eggs, adding bacon and sausage, then a slice of toast.

"Hungry?" asked Dana as she added a couple of slices of bacon to her own plate.

Becca glanced from her plate to Dana's.

"You might want to eat more now and go light at lunch."

Skepticism filled Dana's face. "Not all of us can eat anything we want."

"Yeah, right."

Dana's chin dropped. Becca saw the compressed lips and frown. Unsure why Dana was angry, she sought a way to repair the abrupt silence.

"We're runners, right? Will run for cookies and all that?" Becca kept her voice light and playful as she tried to defuse the sullen tension.

Dana waited several seconds to answer her and when she did, her features stayed fixed.

"You remember Jackie Carlisle?"

She shook her head as they moved down to the beverages, and Becca reached for an orange juice. She tried to figure out how to balance a glass of milk, too.

"Never mind, she was Washington, you wouldn't know her. About the best runner in the state by her sophomore year and got slower every year after that, barely top ten by her senior year, all because she grew."

"So you're not going to grow? Good luck with that."

"Easy for you to say." Anger reddened Dana's cheeks. "Running is my chance to get to college."

The words triggered resentment in Becca but also some guilt as she thought of the letters from coaches around the country trying to recruit her into their programs. Her dad had finally put a stop to the daily text messaging but the letters and phone calls came, regular as clockwork, each promising to make her a better runner and pointing out how much she could help their teams.

It was overwhelming.

They wandered to a table against a far wall, setting the trays down before unloading their plates on to the table and settling down on the long benches. They shifted the trays out of the way and Dana started eating.

"It's not easy for any of us." Becca's voice was soft, and she kept her head down, staring at the mounds of food on her plate. "We're never fast enough, even the kids in front, and they keep pushing us to go faster, work harder, when sometimes all we want to do is run." She glanced at Dana, finding the other girl staring at her. "What?"

"You're hilarious." Dana's voice was flat, and her eyes denied any humor.

Becca reddened, and she attacked a piece of bacon with her fork rather than respond.

"I *saw* you," said Dana. "People that just want to run do three miles on a treadmill or go around the block. At the Foot Locker regional you were pissed because you didn't win." The younger girl leaned her elbows on the table, getting closer to Becca. "So don't feed me any crap about just wanting to run. You want to win."

The black hair danced as Dana gave a hard shake of her head.

"You know, I know I'm not the fastest girl out there. You already proved that you're faster than me; I get it. And girls that I used to beat by a mile are a lot closer and getting faster and I'm not. But I run my butt off trying, and I've got a shot to make it to college; maybe not one of the big programs, but college. In my family, that's a big frickin' deal because none of us have ever gone."

She glanced enviously at Becca's plate.

"Coach keeps trying to help and he's done a good job, I think, always telling me the same things. Be patient, train smart, which is great except I've gained ten pounds in the last year and it's not in spots that make me fast."

Becca's eyes flicked down, and then back up to meet Dana's eyes. She didn't have exactly the same . . . *problem,* she thought self-consciously. Her mom was willowy and Becca took that from her and, while she envied the curviness of other girls, she couldn't imagine trying to run like that. Not that she hadn't developed at all; just, at sixteen, she understood that she'd never have the cleavage the women on the covers of magazines displayed. Becca caught Dana staring at her and her face warmed.

"Yeah, it's like that," said Dana, as though she could read Becca's musings.

Dana paused and dodged back onto safe ground.

"We don't come to camps like this 'just to run.' We show up because we've got something on the line."

Becca shot Dana a fast, thankful glance, happier and far more comfortable talking about running. "I never get told to be patient, it's always *'don't quit'* or *'you only get one shot at this so make it count.' 'There are no second chances, Becca.'* " She was biting out the words. She felt pain radiating up her arm and looked down at her hand, the right one, holding the fork, and unclenched her fist.

"Everything is part of a training plan. Want to go play on a trail? Doesn't fit the plan—today is twenty by four hundred with a two-hundred recovery. Want to do a long run? It's not Sunday, so keep it short and easy instead. Want to lounge around and hang out with the other guys today? Too bad, you're going to run the mountain instead." Her fork clattered on the plate as she dropped it and sat back on the bench. A couple of girls at a nearby table glanced over, then returned to their own conversation. "So yeah, sometimes all I want to do is run." She glared at Dana.

"Sometimes," said Dana. "So what do you want the rest of the time?"

"You always this pushy?"

"I have three little brothers and no mom," said Dana. "It's a habit."

"It's annoying."

Even as she said it, Becca felt the pull of her own mother and missed her. While they were at the camp, her mom was at a conference halfway across the country. Only a week, but it left Becca without her anchor, the person who didn't judge her by the latest race or workout. A life without her . . .

Dana's lips twitched, not quite a smirk but close. Becca saw it and frowned.

"What now?"

"Sharks."

Becca gazed at her, perplexed, so Dana explained.

"My littlest brother, when he doesn't want to talk about something, always talks about sharks."

Becca weighed the words. She knew what she wanted, but she had only told three other people.

One had laughed—her father.

The second, her mom, hugged her and said, "We'll see."

The last, Joseph, had tilted his head in that wise way he had and had said with sympathy, "It's a hard thing you want, Rebecca."

It was one of two secrets she'd shared with Joseph.

She glanced across the room and saw the young Kenyan man step in through the door, framed by slashing sunlight that illuminated his wiry, muscular frame. Behind him, the boys piled in. He let them slide past him as they rushed the food line. His calm gaze scanned the room, lighting briefly on her, long enough to deliver a smile, before continuing his survey.

Joseph had only brought up the first secret once, two years ago, after the first Nationals, when he saw how dejected she was and quietly encouraged her to keep striving, not to quit on her dream. To her relief, he had never mentioned the second secret to her again. She felt her face get warm just thinking about it, about being a silly twelve-year-old girl.

Jim Eagle strode past the doorway, looking as solid as his nickname, "Iron."

Her father was last in and looked haggard and hollow-eyed from a lack of sleep. He had lost half the night on another run to Missoula. Becca still hadn't had a chance to pump Joseph for information. Her dad's eyes slid over her, and gave her a flicker of a smile before moving on. Becca didn't return the smile. She started talking again, without taking her eyes off her father.

"I want to be better than him."

Dana followed Becca's eyes to Rob Hawthorne. "Your dad?"

"He had a shot and missed. I'm not going to miss." Hard determination reflected in her eyes.

"Miss what? You're kinda talking in code and not making a whole lot of sense, girlfriend."

In a flat statement that accepted no contradiction, Becca said, "I'm going to the Olympics." She kept her gaze on Dana and waited while the other girl processed the information.

"Holy crap." Dana let her breath out in a gush. "I thought I had big plans. I just wanted to get to college." She was shaking her head. "You want to race the world."

Becca's lips curled.

"I can do it."

Her eyes turned back to her father.

"If he'll get out of my way."

Chapter 4

"I just don't get why we have to run with girls," said a tall blond runner in a stage whisper to his buddy, a short, freckled guy who looked embarrassed.

Becca blew him off and kept walking but Dana, indignant, stopped and stomped back, two rosy patches showing under her olive complexion. Becca sighed, spun around, and followed Dana.

"What the hell is that supposed to mean?" said Dana as she approached Jazz Harrison. The blond runner smirked at her, his eyes flicking down her body.

Becca tugged her by the elbow. "Come on."

"In a sec," she said, hard and angry, as she pulled free and turned to face Jazz. "Got a problem with girls?" She glanced at the other boy, then back to Jazz. "Don't like them, maybe?" Her smile was sardonic and the words dripped with derision.

Jazz colored and his freckled friend, Tyler, looked at him, face flushed. "Dude, drop it," he said. He turned to Dana and apologized for him. "He didn't mean nothing. Sorry."

"I don't need you talking for me," said Jazz, staring his buddy down. He faced Dana, ignoring Becca. "This is supposed to be an elite camp but so far it's been nothing but lectures and easy runs. We finally get to bust loose and get some real work done and instead, we get to run with girls." He looked straight at Dana. "You'll never keep up."

Becca felt herself get tense and took a couple of fast breaths to calm herself. While she tried to get her anger under control, Dana started talking, her words clipped and sharp. She spoke with an accent now, a flavor of sound that reminded Becca of the itinerant workers that passed through during the summers, men mostly, with dusty clothes, headed to the next harvest.

"The girls will never keep up with those big strong boys?" she said, stepping in toward Jazz's chest. Surprised, he backed up at the invasion of his personal space, and she advanced again. "Maybe the big dumb boys need to learn better manners. Maybe the boys think too much of themselves."

"You can't hang and that's a fact." Jazz's face flushed with anger. "You don't have the muscle to run those hills with us."

Tyler shook his head and Becca shot a glance his way. He clearly wanted to be anywhere else and she felt a flash of sympathy for him. His friend was a jerk but Tyler seemed okay—for a friend of a jerk, at least. In the distance, she saw Eagle check out the group. He frowned but turned back to the impromptu staff meeting he was having.

"We can't hang with the big strong boys because we don't have enough muscles? Did you really say that?" Dana laughed and, in a quick motion, stepped forward and thumped him with her shoulder and upper arm like a hockey player body checking an opposing skater. Shocked at the contact, he retreated another step. Dana laughed again without humor, and said, "You might be right, *pendejo,* I can't hang. We'll find out. But"—she pointed to Becca with a tilt of her head—"see that little girl?"

Jazz's wide eyes slid to Becca and back to the Hispanic girl parked under his chin. Dana started speaking again before he could open his mouth.

"That little girl, *pendejo?* I've seen how she can run." Dana's thick, dark hair swayed as she shook her head. "I worry about you, I do. How is the big strong boy going to handle it when a girl kicks his ass?"

Becca felt her eyes get as wide as Jazz's, and she struggled to avoid laughing at the dumbstruck look on the boy's face. Dana backed away from the boy, a small sweet smile still on her face in contrast to the biting tone she had used to dissect Jazz.

"Dana," said Becca, "we need to get our gear together." She watched fury begin building in Jazz's features as the initial shock passed. Tyler was reaching for him.

"Dude, let it go," he said, and shot a glance Becca's way, almost pleading for help.

Dana let Becca lead her in the direction of their cabin but not before she gave Jazz another contemptuous look, complete with a snort and a flip of her hair. Behind them, Tyler was still talking to Jazz, urging him to cool it. Becca didn't talk until they were well out of earshot.

"You must have a lot of friends."

"Sometimes boys need to be reminded of their manners," said Dana. She looked at Becca and grinned. "My brothers are much bigger pain-in-the-butts."

Becca felt a flash of empathy for Dana's brothers and, in the same flash, really heard Dana's voice.

"What happened to the accent?"

Dana laughed. "Street talk."

Her voice changed and she slid into a swagger. "Gonna talk on the street, best talk like you belong, *sí*? And boys, they think they like crazy until they meet crazy." She looked at Becca again, this time dropping the accent and her defenses. "Not every place is quiet and easy like here. Some places have bad people. The gangs are bad, bad news and they own the schools." She looked past the cabins and the river and the mountains as her voice took on a wistful touch. "I want to come to someplace like this, where I can be me. I want my brothers to come here where I don't have to worry about them."

Becca had no answer for this, so they walked together without speaking. Dana broke the silence first.

"Sorry."

"For what?"

"He's going to go after you, you know."

Becca nodded. "Yeah, I know." She smiled a bit. "Don't worry about it."

"He's mad."

"Well, you were swearing at him so I guess you were, too," said Becca. "What did that mean, anyway?"

"*Pendejo*?"

Becca stopped at the doorway to their cabin and nodded.

"Jackass or asshole," said Dana. "Close enough, at least. It's not really swearing but it isn't very nice."

Becca frowned. "My dad would not approve."

Dana chuckled as she pushed the door open. "Neither would mine." She walked over to her bunk and flopped down onto it.

"So what are you going to do?"

"About the cussing? Nothing." Becca sounded puzzled. "Why would I?"

"About the boys."

Becca smiled at Dana, and her tone was light, but there was a strong undercurrent of excitement. "I'm just going to run with them, no biggie." Dana watched as Becca stared out the window and up into the mountains. Becca's voice became predatory. "I own the trails."

Becca added a small first-aid kit, a snack, a whistle, some waterproof matches, a short but strong piece of slender rope, and a bandana to her small run pack and hefted it, checking for balance.

Dana watched her prepare and looked glumly at her own pack—borrowed from the staff and only loosely filled—and said, "I thought we were going on a run, not on a reenactment of the Lewis and Clark expedition."

Becca didn't look up as she scoured the bottom of her gear bag. "It's mountain trails. Crap happens." She stood the bag on end as she searched around her spare clothing. "Ha! Got it," she said, and withdrew a small knife.

"What do you need that for?"

"Bears," said Becca with a straight face.

Dana looked at her dubiously, and Becca burst into laughter.

"That's not very funny," said Dana, sounding defensive.

Becca glanced at Dana with a perceptive eye. "Have you ever been trail running? I mean, not in a park or anything, but out here, where the wild things are."

Dana smiled. "That was my favorite book when I was a little kid."

"Yeah, well, out here there really are wild things." Seeing Dana's body tensing, Becca said, "Mostly they'll run away if they hear us coming." Dana's shoulders relaxed, but she still fidgeted with her hands.

"Would you relax?" said Becca as she stuffed the knife into her pack. "Let me see what you got." She reached for Dana's fanny pack and quickly rifled through the meager contents while Dana watched. Becca tossed the bag back to her, and her hands disappeared into the gear bag again.

"I have some extras," she said, pulling out a purple bandana and another length of the rope. She handed them to Dana, who dutifully put them in the bag. Becca looked apologetic. "I don't have another knife or first-aid kit but if you were running by yourself, you should have them."

Dana, eyes still a bit large, nodded. "You learn this at camp last year?"

Becca smile and gave her an amused look. "My dad, when I was about eight."

"Eight?"

The amused look became a rueful grin. "It's Montana. The bears come to you out here. You learn to be ready." She grabbed her water bottle. "Come on, let's go get checked in."

Rob Hawthorne checked Becca's run pack and handed it back to her. A few feet away, Eagle was doing the same with his cadre of runners.

"Looks good," Rob said. Indecision crossed his face, and then cleared as he regained his normal assurance. Under his breath, he added, "Jim said there was some commotion after lunch." A practiced glance checked Becca's water bottle, and he looked directly at her. "Trust your instincts," he said, voice far softer than his eyes, surprising her, as he moved to Dana.

As her father moved to one of the boys, Becca watched Joseph emerge from the lodge, walking, almost strolling in his fluid way, to the small sandy beach at the edge of the river.

"Be back in a sec," she said to Dana, and jogged in his direction. Joseph saw her coming and a cautious smile appeared as he slowed.

"Hello, Rebecca," he said as she came within earshot. "It looks as though you are leaving soon. The others are envious."

Becca snorted. "I wouldn't mind lounging in the water, but I got a date with some boys."

Joseph nodded understandingly. "The rumors are spreading." He started moving toward the water and she stepped beside him.

"So why has Dad been going to Missoula? Every time he comes back, he goes right to you and you end up looking like someone stepped on your puppy."

The corners of his mouth twitched slightly. "I do not have a puppy," he said without looking at her.

"You are such a brat," said Becca. "You know what I mean."

A shout interrupted them before she could press him more for answers. "Becca," Eagle called over, "let's go."

Joseph touched her arm. "It is not bad news. Your father is trying to do a favor for me, a hard one." He hesitated, clearly uncertain as to how much to reveal.

"Remember my cousin?" He glanced toward Eagle. "I have told you about her?"

Becca remembered and nodded. Joseph had told her about Grace, a girl who loved to run in a country that expected almost half of the women to be married before they turned sixteen. She vaguely recalled that Grace was three or four years younger than her. With a start, she realized that in the distant regions of Kenya, Grace was moving into prime marriageable age, and her eyes widened.

Joseph nodded.

"Your father is trying to bring her to this country, but her family does not want her to leave. They have negotiated a marriage," he explained, distaste flowing with the words, "and wish to ensure that they will receive a better income before they allow her to leave, to go to Nairobi and then here, to the United States."

"Becca," Eagle shouted again, "you're holding up the bus."

She tried to comprehend the idea that sounded suspiciously as though the family in Kenya was trying to *sell* their daughter.

Becca looked at Joseph, undecided, and then turned. "I got to go."

He gave her a shrewd look. "Trust him," he said, shifting subjects. "Your father tries very hard for you."

"I—"

"Becca!" Eagle shouted, and started to walk toward her, a frown on his face as he shifted his gaze from her to Joseph and back.

She hastened toward the trail runners.

"Rebecca." She turned to look at Joseph while the others waited. He glanced at the sky as a peculiar look crossed his face. "Be careful."

An unsettled feeling wormed its way around her insides, but she nodded as she tried to process the idea that her dad was trying to bring another girl into their house.

Another girl runner.

Chapter 5

Becca inspected the "bridge" carefully. Next to her, Dana did the same, with growing apprehension that was shared by several of the other runners.

Three ropes spanned the river, tied to trees on the far bank and a wood stockade on this side. A puff of wind sent a soft shimmy along the ropes as the center swayed out, reaching in the direction of a gray log balanced on a lichen-covered boulder a dozen feet or so downriver. The ten-foot-long log was suspended eight feet above the water that relentlessly beat on the rock, a testament to both the incredible power and patience of the river. One day the river would regain its bit of driftwood.

"Listen up, people," said Eagle. He looked at the group to make sure that he had their attention.

"The rules don't change just because we're out of camp. In fact, they're even more important, plus we're going to add a couple. First, this is a team effort. That means that nobody goes off on their own. You maintain contact with the other runners on your team.

"Second, this isn't a race. Once we cross the river, you're going to be running on trails, real trails, not those groomed things they have in city parks. It's a totally different environment for most of you. You have to be constantly aware of your surroundings. There's no telling what might come popping out of the woods. One thing to pay attention to is the trail. Keep an eye out for rattlesnakes, especially down by the river."

Becca felt her skin getting moist from the heat of the sun, the sweat mixing with the fine dust that settled on everything after the vans had rolled to a stop. She wiped her face with her bandana while sizing up the effect of Eagle's speech on the group.

Jazz looked bored, but most of the runners, including Dana, were covering up a bad case of nerves with strained smiles and uncertain glances at the thinness of the ropes suspended above the river. The sound of the water provided background noise but the air was still except for the usual little noises from the squirrels and birds. Becca looked at the bridge and the rock shelf on the other side of the river and felt a small thrill run through her. She looked back to Eagle as he started talking again.

"We're heading out in two groups to keep this manageable. Coach Hawthorne won the toss, so he's taking his gang up the ridge," he said, pointing up toward the mountaintops, "to a lake about four miles out."

Jazz glanced up the mountain, his eyes following the direction of the coach's pointing finger. Tyler, standing next to him in a scrap of shade, did the same but without the same nonchalance.

"It doesn't sound that far, but you're at altitude and it's hot. Keep the pace down and hydrate. The folks with me are headed up along the river a couple of miles before we turn uphill."

The runners were nodding, so Eagle continued.

"First, though, we have to cross the bridge. It's easier than you think *if* you follow our instructions. If you don't, we're packing everybody up and headin' back." He looked around the group to confirm that they understood—the teamwork started on this side of the bridge.

"Okay, good. Coach Hawthorne is going to demonstrate how to cross."

Becca smothered a chuckle, and Dana glanced at her quizzically. "Tell you later," said Becca under her breath, a twisted smile making her eyes light up.

Eagle kept talking while the runners began to shuffle a bit. "We'll go one at a time. Be patient—the rope will amplify any motions that you make, so slow and steady as you cross."

Rob Hawthorne was already walking to the bridge, a safety line tied to his waist. Their end of the bridge was anchored by the wooden stockade, a beefy system of logs, cross-braced against each other and deeply buried in the gritty soil. They leaned slightly toward the river, victims of erosion, as nature relentlessly reclaimed her own against the best efforts of mere humans. The far end was attached to tall lodgepole pines just above a semicircle of sandy beach.

Hawthorne eased out onto the bottom rope, using his hands to grasp the two lines that formed the top of the V-shaped bridge. The rope sagged under his weight, and the angle of the rope changed, becoming steeper. He turned, feet splayed and pointing up the rope, almost gripping the knots of the thinner ropes that tied the hand ropes to the bottom, walking rope.

"The first rule is easy. Don't panic," he said, and smiled, standing relaxed. His voice, softer than Jim Eagle's, was calm without being cool. "The ropes are going to move, so stay relaxed and work with them. I like to keep my feet angled a bit so

I don't have to shift my weight all the way around my foot as I walk." He took two backwards steps, demonstrating. "See how it keeps the hips opened up? That should help a bit with balance as you cross."

"*Right* . . ." Tyler muttered. Jazz smirked at him.

Becca stayed focused on her father, observing the transitions in weight and building a mental picture of herself on the rope. Her stomach clenched, and she took a cleansing breath. Dana's elbow caught her in the arm, and she looked over.

"You haven't done this?" asked Dana.

"Nuh-uh."

Rob turned and started to traverse the rope and the sag increased as he crossed over the bank. Becca could see the rounded rock through the water below his feet. He was more careful turning around this time, and the bridge quivered and rocked.

"I thought you'd done the mountain run thing before."

"Yeah," said Becca, "but we used a proper bridge farther up the river." She glanced at Dana. "Like twenty miles up. This is new."

"Great," replied Dana as Rob finished his turn.

"The water isn't deep out at this point but you also have the farthest to fall. On the plus side, the water's warm this late in the season." His joke didn't get any laughs.

"As you cross, stay steady and focus on balance. Keep your knees relaxed and don't get in a hurry. Don't forget to breathe. You'll feel it when you get to the halfway mark because the angle on the ropes will start heading up. It's a bit easier to go up than down but it's also easy to get in too much of a rush to get off the bridge. *Don't hurry.*"

He turned, using gradual changes, and proceeded to the far bank. As he walked, the bottom rope dropped until it was only six feet above the surface of the burbling water. He changed the angle of his body as he started up the other side, smoothly shifting his feet. He cleared the river and finished at the trees, stepping off as he got to the last knot. He ducked under the hand rope and untied the safety line.

"Okay, who wants to try this first?" he shouted across the river as he belayed the rope around the closest tree.

"Me," said Jazz, striding confidently to the ropes.

"Slow down there, big guy," said Eagle. In his right hand he held a bright orange safety harness. "First, you're going to put this on."

"I don't need it," the youth said.

"Good for you, but everybody here is going to wear it anyway." Jim scanned the group and a broad smile broke out on his face. "Yeah, it's a bit on the scary side, but none of you are going to land in the water." He lifted the harness so they could all see the details of it. "See this clip? It's rated for one thousand pounds. The rope is rated for seven hundred. We'll have you anchored on both shores." The smile ignited again. "So breathe, people. Come on over, Jazz, and we'll show everybody how this goes on."

In less than a minute, Jazz was outfitted and ready. He ducked under the rope and stepped up.

"Out nice and easy, Jazz," said Eagle.

Becca watched Jazz slide out onto the rope, using the same bent-knee gait her father had. The sag below him increased as he moved over the river but the bottom rope was steady with only little movements as he shifted his weight. Jazz bobbled a bit as he headed back up the rope but he steadied it by dropping a little deeper at his knees. Motion quieted, he eased up to the other bank and stepped off next to Becca's dad as comfortably as if he were stepping off the porch of his house.

". . . *overachiever*. . ." muttered Tyler. He looked almost ill, head hanging down and his shoulders collapsed around his ears. On the far bank, Jazz exchanged words with Becca's father. Rob nodded and smiled.

"Okay, who's next?" asked Eagle as he retracted the harness along the safety line.

"Me," said Dana, thrusting ahead of another of the boys, practically elbowing him in the gut.

"Good job, Dana," said Eagle and started guiding her into the harness, cinching it down a bit snugger to fit her smaller frame. He gave her a reassuring grin as she gingerly put one foot up on the rope.

"It's all about balance—"

"Oh good," Dana said, looking at her feet. "Balance I can do. It's swimming I'm not too sure about."

Eagle laughed, low and amused, and said, "You'll do just fine. Relax and don't forget to breathe out there."

She looked up with a fast smile. "Right."

She walked out on the rope, adapting to the slope. There was a steady vibration as Dana constantly adjusted her weight. Becca watched how the other girl shifted around the knots and practiced visualizing herself out on the rope, feeling it across the arches of her feet, the rough texture of the hand ropes sliding past her fingers.

Just past halfway, a gust of wind caught Dana mid-step, and she floundered against the hand ropes, trying to get her other foot down. Eagle and Rob Hawthorne braced themselves, prepared to take the slack if she started to fall. After an eternal full undulation of the rope, she recovered her footing and, without a pause, resumed walking. She crossed over the bank and, three steps later, almost jumped off the rope.

Even from the other side of the river, Becca could hear the triumphant "HA!" from Dana as the other girl thrust her arms in the air in celebration, getting high fives from Rob and Jazz. The other runners laughed, and the one that Dana had elbowed moved forward to take his turn.

One by one, they crossed until just Becca was left.

"Ready?" asked Eagle.

"Yep," said Becca, knowing how to put on the harness from watching, and doing so without help. She cinched the harness a bit too tightly, so she loosened it at the shoulders.

Becca took a deep breath before mounting the bridge. The rope felt a bit thicker underfoot than she had imagined. She felt the little quivers through her soles as the wind, picking up, exerted itself against the flimsy structure. Becca relaxed and flowed out onto the rope, keeping her eyes focused at the far end while she trusted her feet to sense the rope and adapt. A gust of wind hit her nearly at the same point as it had hit Dana, but she had both feet down and unconsciously turned her hips to minimize her profile. The whole bridge swayed out and she leaned to keep the rope centered under her.

She paused twice more for wind, waiting patiently for stability. When she stepped off on the other side of the bridge, she was coated in sweat from more than the summer heat.

"Nicely done," said her father.

She knew, in a corner of her mind that wasn't involved in balancing precariously over the water, that Jazz had watched her. He met her eyes as she untangled herself from the harness and gave a grudging flip of his head to acknowledge her. She gave him an expressionless stare before looking away.

On the other side of the river, Eagle was setting himself on the bridge. From the instant his feet hit rope, Becca could see the vibrations. The normally surefooted coach swayed and fought to maintain his balance as he crossed. At mid-span, a stronger gust of wind hit him, and she could see him mouth a low obscenity but the sound carried away from them on the wind, drowned by the sounds of the river. He recovered and continued.

"What's so funny?" Dana asked.

Becca realized she was grinning, and it blossomed into a full smile. "Coach Eagle."

Dana looked at her uncomprehendingly.

Becca nearly laughed and a couple of the runners from Eagle's group glanced in their direction. "His nickname is Iron, right?"

Dana nodded. "The boys said he must have been a pilot or something, like the movie."

"Nope," she said. "I don't think he was ever a pilot. My dad or Coach would have told me." She gave Dana a sidelong glance. "You ever see him in the water at the beach?" she asked, referring to the slender stretch of sand along the river at camp.

Dana shook her head, her eyes slipping from Becca to Eagle, who was nearly over. Becca waited until Dana was looking at her again before she finished her story.

"I've known Coach Eagle my whole life, nearly," she said, "and I've never seen him swimming." Her smile got bigger and she nodded to the coach as he stepped off the bridge. "He got his nickname for how well he floats."

Comprehension lit up in Dana's eyes. "Oh," was all she said.

Becca shrugged. "I bet you that he was at least as worried about that bridge as we were." She looked at Dana with amusement tinged with understanding.

"The Iron Eagle doesn't like water."

Chapter 6

Becca walked to the bank of the river and dampened her bandana, tying it loosely around her throat. The clear, cold water ran down her back, leaving a wet spot on her shirt.

Eagle's runners gathered around him while Becca walked back toward her dad. Rob and the others started walking to the edge of the clearing. Becca could see the single-track trail snaking out ahead of them as she merged in next to Dana. Dana still retained the flush of excitement from the crossing.

"That was totally cool," Dana said. Tyler was nodding his head, but Jazz just gave her a half smirk.

"It was okay," he said.

"Well, you're a party-pooper," she said. She tried to sound cross but her natural exuberance bubbled out. "Maybe for you or Becca, it happens all the time, but this"—she swept an arm around to embrace the trees and cliff, almost thumping Tyler in the chest—"is kind of incredible."

"There's not much like this around Corvallis," said Tyler. "Eagle Scout here—"

"I'm not an Eagle Scout yet," said Jazz, frowning at his friend, adding somewhat defensively. "It's tougher to do than you think."

Tyler continued as though he had never been interrupted. "—gets out into the mountains but we're in the Willamette Valley.'" He shrugged. "Mostly, I know how to run with wet feet all the time."

Becca sneaked a glance at Jazz. He didn't look like much of an Eagle Scout to her. He strode alongside the group but slightly apart, and radiated nervous energy.

He's ready to go, thought Becca, and felt the usual queasiness in her stomach. It was like this before every race, totally confident until the race closed in and then a catalogue of possible problems fluttered into her head, upsetting her stomach. She took a steadying breath. Jazz saw it and he smiled, his lips thinning and no warmth hitting his eyes.

She took a sip from her water bottle, rolling it around her mouth before swallowing. She could feel the parched air sucking moisture from her pores even as a gust of wind snatched the sweat from the skin. She knew from experience that the sun would roast them as soon as they cleared the trees. She also knew that Jazz hadn't used his bottle yet; he was already dehydrating from the combination of altitude and heat. She could use that.

"Drink up, everybody, and let's get going," said Rob. "We have two hours to get up to the lake and back."

"You said it's only four miles," said Jazz. "We can do that easy." He stared at Becca as he talked, but she kept her eyes on her dad.

"Four miles uphill, and some of these are bomber climbs. Plus it's hot and going to get hotter in the sun, and weather is supposed to roll in later this afternoon. We want to be back at camp before it gets here." He looked around at his charges. "Here's the deal. If I see any of you not sweating, all of us turn around. Up the side of a mountain is a hell of a place to get heat-stroke so we're not going to take any chances."

Becca watched as the information sank into the group. Dana was the first to take a sip, but both boys followed quickly. Becca checked her bottle; still mostly full but she knew that she'd be out by the top of the hill.

"Any chance of refilling at the lake?" she asked her dad.

"You brought your iodine tablets?"

She made a face. The water always had a weird tang after being treated with the chemical, but the iodine made it reasonably safe to drink.

Dana looked over to the sparkling water rushing past as she adjusted her run pack, trying to get it to settle on her hips so it wouldn't rub.

"What's wrong with the water?"

"Nothing," said Becca. "We just—"

"The deer crap in it," interrupted Jazz. "You can get giardiasis if you're not careful."

Dana looked at Becca for reassurance. Becca made a rueful face and shrugged.

"We've been swimming in it."

Rob chuckled. "Jazz is right, but you generally have to drink the water." He paused, almost as an afterthought. "And pretty much nothing in life is risk-free."

Dana looked to the river again, and Becca laughed. "Welcome to where the wild things are," she said.

"I missed this part in the book," said Dana.

Rob smiled and pointed to the trail. "Come on, let's start

moving. Keep it really easy until everybody is warmed up. And"—he looked at Becca and Jazz—"for you hotshots, old man Coach Hawthorne slow, not your slow."

Eagle's group was still getting organized as one by one they slipped out onto the trail, following Hawthorne. In seconds, the clearing was lost behind a turn and tall, slender pines.

The trail switchbacked up out of the river valley and all the runners were soaked with sweat within a few minutes. The footing was good, earthy with the detritus of the trees softening the impact on their feet and only a few rocks so far. From what Becca remembered of the topo map, they would top out about five hundred feet above the river and the trail would follow the mostly wooded ridge up to the alpine area with the lake. She glanced to her right and caught a reflection of the sun off the silver ribbon of the river as it snaked away. She pointed as she ran.

"Pretty," said Dana, not wasting words. She sounded winded.

Ahead, the boys ran, Jazz with a powerful stride that looked to overpower the trail, Tyler struggling a bit to keep up. Becca watched as Jazz pushed off a rock too aggressively and it dislodged, causing him to lurch forward to recover his balance. She filed it away.

She ran lightly, adjusting her own stride to compensate for the rocks and roots as she came to them, seeking the most efficient path up the hill. Years of her dad badgering her to "run tall" showed in the line of her form as she moved nimbly.

"Run taller," said her dad's voice behind her, and a flash of annoyance filled her before she realized that he was talking to Dana. "It opens up your lungs to get more air."

"Right," said the other girl.

Ahead, Tyler straightened up a bit as well and his arm carriage improved immediately.

They cleared another switchback and the trail straightened and flattened, with the top still out of sight. Jazz started to accelerate away.

"Jazz, hold up, bud," called Hawthorne. He was dropping down to a walk, breathing heavily but steadily. Becca tipped her head as her gaze sharpened on him. He met her eyes with an impassive look.

"Water break," he said as the boy came jogging back.

Becca took a sip and then another, letting the last one swish around her mouth and cleanse it. Her breathing steadied quickly and she felt loose-limbed and relaxed. The scent of the trees wafted around them and she relaxed into the familiarity of the scene. A scurrying sound came from the uphill side of the trail. She turned her gaze to the brush in time to see a chipmunk dodge under a rock for protection from the intruders—and possible predators.

"We have about a half mile of fairly flat ground before we head up again. Once we hit the next hill, we'll be exposed to a lot of sun. Take that into account as we go. If you want to spread out some, go for it. The trail is going to get rocky in spots so watch your footing."

With Jazz leading again, the group jogged on. The western larch, western white pine, and lodgepole pines in the valley yielded to spruce and towering lodgepoles. Ahead was a scattering of twinberry flowers, delicate purple blooms at the edges of the trail, the kind she used to pick when she was much younger and the "runs" were hikes and an adventure. As they reached the end of the level stretch, the trees began to take on a withered look, many of them barren of foliage. The vegetation below the canopy thickened with the added sunlight.

"Fire?" guessed Tyler, throwing the words over his shoulder in Hawthorne's general direction. Like Dana, he was having trouble with the altitude and was running conservatively.

"Beetles," said the coach, calling ahead. "Big problem all over the Pacific Northwest. The Forest Service is working on it but it's probably the worst outbreak they've seen."

The gaps between the trees grew, and Becca felt the naked sun's heat cooking her shoulder where her sleeveless top exposed her tanned skin. Ahead, the trees petered out at a rock outcropping and the trail looped in front of it, turning sharply uphill. She took another long sip of water as she ran, holding up the bottle to see how much she had left. A strong gust of wind filtered through the trees, rustling the branches with a high, lonely sigh. Ahead, Jazz burst into full sunlight onto the rocky stretch Rob had forewarned them of. He looked over his shoulder, back at Becca . . . and accelerated.

Anger stirred in her stomach and tension in her shoulders blossomed. Ahead, Tyler was shaking his head as he crossed into the sun.

Her dad's voice drifted up, low enough that only she and Dana could hear it. "Sometimes you just have to go for it, seize the chance."

The anger exploded inside. Only in her dad's world were there no second chances. The former standout runner–*who quit when he didn't make the Olympics*–accused everybody else of quitting. She saw Jazz digging in on the rocky terrain and, for a brief instant, contemplated letting him go, but even as she thought it, her turnover increased and she surrendered to instinct.

Another gust of wind buffeted her and the sun disappeared behind a fast-moving, towering cloud. She cleared the trees, passing Tyler as he slowed. He speared her with a perplexed look that she refused to acknowledge when she flowed past him.

Her fiery, determined eyes were locked on the back of Jazz.

Chapter 7

The hot, gusting wind bounced Becca sideways, but she adapted, altering her landing position slightly on the rocky trail to flow with it. Eight feet in front of her, Jazz was forced to change his stride to hang on to his balance.

Becca could feel the burn in her lungs from the mile-long chase to catch up to Jazz. She channeled her anger into patient, focused effort, selecting each step quickly but with care. The sweat was flowing off in rivulets, but she couldn't spare the attention to snatch another drink of water. Her sunglasses barely cut the glare off the granite rock that created stark contrasts on the trail, each rock and chunk of rubble throwing its own shadow, making it difficult to judge solid footing from sudden treachery.

Ahead, Jazz grunted as he slipped again. The back of Becca's mind analyzed the runner ahead, took note of his strength and speed. He stubbornly continued to apply brute force to the trail and she could see the strain building from his efforts. She nimbly sidestepped the dislodged rock. She watched his feet, seeing the way Jazz was toeing off on his push up the ridge.

His feet have gone flat, she thought, as Jazz began using more and more quad and hamstring muscles instead of calves to elevate up the mountain. The thought gave her satisfaction. She closed another couple of feet. His struggling effort to speed up and his gasping breaths told her that he knew she was close on his heels. She continued to push him while she waited for a place to demolish him.

Rob Hawthorne watched his daughter gracefully traverse a technical section of the trail even as her whole body radiated her anger. The two runners were more than a quarter mile ahead of them now. Rob dropped his pace a bit. Dana and Tyler slowed with him.

"She's like a mountain goat," said Dana, looking up at the slim figure of Becca pursuing Jazz. The freshman was dripping wet and huffing.

"She spends her summers on trails. We live up in the hills so it's easy for her to just bolt out the door. In five minutes, she's in the woods."

Tyler looked up the exposed ridge at the two figures, Jazz's blue singlet standing out with Becca's vivid yellow.

"Jazz is still winning."

"Why did you let them race?" asked Dana.

Rob ran gently, his feet barely disturbing the ground. A mix of thoughts swirled through his head on how to answer the question. He glanced back up the hill as Becca and Jazz crested the ridge. He knew the trail would flatten again before a last hard climb to the lake.

"Because they both needed to learn something," he finally said. He didn't elaborate.

The three of them ran in silence. Rob could hear their feet pounding on the trail. He slowed down even more.

"Listen," he said.

"To what?" asked Tyler.

Rob didn't answer.

"I can hear birds and stuff," said Dana, breathing easier with the reduced speed.

"That's not it," said Rob.

They kept running, hitting the base of the same grade that the two leaders had just cleared. Tyler leaned into the hill and slid as a rock scattered out from under his foot.

"Water break," said Rob, pulling up to a stop, feet set at an angle across the trail, the uphill leg bent at the knee to keep him stable. Dana emulated his stance. Tyler braced against a handy boulder. Unlimbering a water bottle from his pack—Hawthorne was carrying two bottles in his sweat-stained run pack—he took a couple of fast gulps. The kids did the same.

From their perch, they could see the sweep of the mountain range, the trees on the mountains on the other side of the river clean and sharply focused in the thin air. The river itself was hidden in the depths below. The mountains in the distance faded into a hazy blue. Rob glanced up as another towering cloud scudded past, breaking the heat of the sun. More clouds were building on the horizon. Vague apprehension that he had made a mistake started gnawing at him.

"What were we listening for?" asked Dana.

Tyler was nodding. "I hear the same stuff," he said, "just birds, and lots of little skittering sounds and the wind."

Rob smiled. "What don't you hear now?"

Both of them listened and Rob watched as the answer percolated into Dana's eyes.

Dana grinned. "Our feet."

Recognition lit up in Tyler's eyes as she spoke.

"Exactly. Both of you were kind of clumping when you run. All that extra noise means you're wasting energy."

"So how do we fix it?" asked Tyler.

"Pretend you're a mountain goat," joked Dana. "Is that what you taught Becca?"

Rob shook his head. "I didn't have to teach her. She's a natural runner. I try to not mess her up too much while helping her get better." A cloud crossed his face and his normal cheerfulness faded for a moment. "It's tough on Becca to have her dad also be her coach."

He saw Dana give him a strange look, much too old for a young lady, as though she were sympathetic. He mentally shrugged.

"Okay, let's get restarted. Walk first and ease into a run. Don't try to monkey with your form too much on the hill. Running quiet is tough on the calves and you'll blow yourself up. Play a little but stay comfortable."

Another cloud crossed the sun and Hawthorne felt a deep anxiety. He looked up the mountain. Jazz and Becca were specks, and they disappeared around a curve high above them. He sighed before settling into a manageable pace, guiding Dana and Tyler upward.

Becca's thighs felt like lead, her lungs ached from the effort to pull oxygen from the thin air, and her eyes hurt from squinting. Still, she was pleased because, just in front of her, Jazz was falling apart. She could taste salt from her lips as she quickly wiped a hand across her face to remove excess sweat.

They were on the last uphill—Becca hoped it was the last— and she was still harassing Jazz from the rear. Running this close to him, with no time to react, was disorienting. He would dodge around or jump over obstacles that she couldn't see until a bare second before she needed to decide how to handle it. Backing off occurred to her, but would mean easing up the pressure Jazz built on himself. She packed in close and waited.

Ahead, Jazz hesitated for a split second, then, slipping again, lurched left. Becca had a brief glimpse of a split in the trail. Her first instinct was to follow Jazz. If she maintained contact until a widening of the track, she could blitz past him before he could react.

But sensing a chance to put Jazz away, she gambled and went right, up a steeper path. Vision clear now, she saw that the side she chose led up and around an outcropping. Already she was several feet higher than Jazz.

Crap, she cursed, angry at herself for taking the chance.

If her side trail didn't tie back to the main trail soon, Jazz would have an insurmountable lead. Committed, she hurled herself at the mountain. The burn in her thighs dialed up from medium to high.

Below her, Jazz put on a burst but sputtered out as he hit a technical stretch of loose scree.

Becca kept her shoulders up, sucking air into tight lungs. Thankfully the sun parked itself behind a bank of clouds and the high outcrop gave her a brief respite from the winds that were pummeling both of them.

The top of the trail forked back to the main trail but on a slight downhill. Jazz was just clearing the scree field and getting back up to speed, surging on the rocky narrow path.

Narrow, with no place to pass.

The trail slipped into a stand of pines a quarter mile farther up that Becca hoped surrounded the lake or she was going to lose to Jazz. She could beat him over the next four hundred meters but if it went much longer . . .

Becca released the brakes and let herself fall down the trail, using gravity to force heavy legs to move faster, feet touching just long enough to lift back off the earth, using the terrain to maintain footing.

She rejoined the main trail with ten yards on Jazz. She heard the scattering rocks as he tried to speed up to catch her but Becca let the momentum of the small downhill carry her up the slope, through the trees and, finally, to the clearing at the lake, still ten yards in front of Jazz.

She drifted to a stop, hands on her hips as she pulled in oxygen. She fought the urge to fold over but her legs were quivering beneath her. She briefly closed her eyes as she thought about her gamble and how narrow the upper trail had been. She let out a long breath and the exiting air made her feel lighter.

She opened her eyes again when she heard Jazz stumble in, wheezing. Looking back, Becca saw him grabbing his knees and coughing, his throat raspy from the hot, dry air at eight thousand feet. Jazz struggled upright again and met her eyes.

Instead of the anger she braced for, his eyes reflected acknowledgement. Then he buckled over again in a paroxysm of coughing.

"You okay?" she asked, surprised that her voice sounded as raspy as his cough.

He was bobbing his head as he coughed and reached for his water bottle. He swigged a couple of fast mouthfuls. The coughing started to subside. With a start, Becca grabbed her bottle and gulped down the now-warm water.

"Yeah," he said as he returned to a fully upright position. He looked out over the lake and the vast open spaces on the other side. "Wow."

Becca turned to look.

The clear water sat in a basin against the mountain on three sides with tall conifers surrounding it. The reflection of overlooking mountains lay on the blue surface in a ripply mirror image, swiftly billowing clouds skimming the surface. Three hundred yards across the lake, she could see two small streams feeding fresh water into the basin, and closer to the shore they stood on, a fish jumped, the water splashing up in clear diamonds as the trout sought a snack. The wavelets floated to them and were subsumed into the whole again.

"That's pretty stinking spectacular," she agreed.

Mentally she kicked herself for forgetting her camera. For all the years that she had gone into the mountains with her dad, she never lost her sense of awe or appreciation of the different personalities of the peaks that cut sharp lines against an azure sky. One would be one grim and foreboding, another shallower sloped and forgiving, often sitting side by side like mismatched brothers. They all shared a common trait, though. Each peak, jagged or craggy or welcoming, looked over their shared domain with an air of permanence. *We endure,* they all whispered to her.

It was here she measured herself, and, in the freedom of their slopes, her spirit soared.

The two competitors stood apart from each other as they gazed over the rock-strewn shore, a stiff breeze cooling their skin. Another fish jumped.

"I'm going to have to come back with my fishing pole," said Jazz. The rasp was fading and he smiled. "But next time, I'll walk up." His hair was plastered down on his scalp and his face was red. The singlet, drenched with sweat, stuck to his torso.

"Be more fun."

"That was fun," said Jazz. "All except the part where you beat me. Did you know that side trail would dump you out ahead of me?"

Becca shook her head. "I haven't been up here before."

The ephemeral words glided into the open air and evaporated. They were silent for a moment, still standing a bit apart. From the corner of her eye, Becca watched as Jazz's face became serious.

"I could beat you on level ground, you know."

It wasn't braggadocio. His words were quiet and calm and matter-of-fact.

"Maybe," said Becca. She tilted her head slightly toward him. "Probably." Her voice matched his.

That seemed enough to satisfy Jazz.

Becca felt the post-race high dissipating and a rumble in her tummy made her mouth begin to water. She dug through her pack, yanking out an energy bar hidden by the first-aid kit, and shredded the wrapper trying to get it opened. She looked over to Jazz.

"Want some?"

"Sure."

She broke the bar in half and extended one part to him with an outstretched arm. He reached over and snagged it, bringing it up and taking a bite.

"Thanks," he said, around the food.

Tyler was the first through the gap in the trees where the trail terminated, closely followed by Dana. Rob brought up the rear.

"So who won?" Tyler asked, almost before he had stopped. Jazz glanced his way but didn't answer.

"She beat you, huh?" Tyler sounded surprised. Dana looked pleased.

"No worries."

Tyler started to add something but Jazz gave a single decisive shake of his head and cut him off.

"She can run." He didn't add anything else, and his tone discouraged further probing.

Rob Hawthorne was next to Tyler, appraising Jazz with an understanding eye. Becca glanced at her dad as Dana walked to the edge of the water, scanning the shoreline all the way around.

Her dad was worried; she could see the signs. A slight furrow in the brow, a pinched look at the eyes, and his lips, normally curled in a good-natured humor, were flat. He pulled the radio off his hip even as his gaze went up to the mountain. Becca tracked his eyes. The clouds were lofting higher and turning dingier, no longer glaring white.

"What's up?"

"Got a bad vibe." He kept his voice soft. "I'm going to try and get hold of Jim. Make sure everybody waters up."

He walked away and she heard the crackle of the radio as he turned it on.

Becca walked over to Dana.

"How are you doing on water?"

Dana held up her bottle. "Not too bad. Maybe half left." Her eyes were sparkling as she viewed the mountains laid in front of them. "You're really lucky."

"Right," said Becca. She gave Dana a wry grin. "It's not like this every day, y'know?"

"Yeah, but still . . . this place has everything."

"Try and find a good sports bra," suggested Becca.

Dana gave a fast, short chuckle. "No such thing."

Becca watched the clouds continue to pile up and speed toward the sun, still high in the afternoon sky. "When you're done drinking, I'll put an iodine tablet in your bottle and you can refill it." She paused. "It'll taste like heck, though."

Becca walked over and passed on the same message to the boys. Jazz held out his bottle.

"I'm dry."

"I've got plenty," said Tyler.

Becca dug back into the depths of her run pack and brought out the little bottle that held the pills for water treatment. She cracked it open, slipped one onto her palm, and gave it to him.

"How long before it's drinkable? We always use filters camping instead."

"About half an hour." She pulled out her bottle and swallowed half the contents, leaving a couple of inches in the bottom. "Finish it up and I'll get mine going, too."

The radio couldn't reach the far valley where the other runners were training. Five minutes after trying to raise Eagle, Rob Hawthorne had his group organized and ready to head back down the ridge. The clouds had covered the sun and, rather than providing refreshing shade, had cast a gloom over the little clearing.

"Let's get rolling, guys," he said. His voice was terse. "Ease into it and mind your footing. When we get to that scree field, I want all of you walking—no twisted ankles today, please. We head down as a group—no one does a run out." He stared at Jazz.

"Okay, Coach," said Jazz, who was standing next to Dana. Then a puzzled look came over his face, and his eyes flew open wide.

Becca felt it at the same time—the fine hairs on her arm and the base of her neck lifting and tingling. Time slowed down as a touch of panic exploded. At the back of her neck, she felt the loose hairs pulling on her ponytail, and the tingling on her skin intensified.

Even as her dad started to shout and fall to the ground, she launched herself at Tyler, who was closest. Out of the corner of her eye, she could see Jazz taking down Dana, could see the uncomprehending look on the girl's face.

Becca's shoulder hammered squarely into Tyler's chest and he fell backward without a sound as Becca rolled away from him with the impact.

Just as Becca hit the pine needles and gritty dirt of the ground, the world erupted into an explosion of light that left wicked traces on her retinas even through the closed lids while a ground-shattering roar assaulted her ears and shook her deep in her bones.

Chapter 8

Becca lay on the ground, dazed from the concussive impact. The reverberations of the thunder left her ears ringing. The smell of ozone hung on the air while spots danced in her vision. Gradually she became aware of a pine needle pricking her cheek like a miniature sword. The point of pain gave her something to focus on, and her madly galloping thoughts slowed.

She heard someone out of sight groan as they tried moving. Becca closed her eyes and lifted herself to hands and knees, more pine needles poking the skin under her palms. She opened her eyes to stare at her hands. Her shoulders and elbows were quivering and an almost irresistible urge to run threatened what little self-control she clung to.

No panicking in the woods . . . bad things happen to people who panic. . . .

To her left, she heard someone–*Dana*–start to cry. Becca scrambled up to a hunched but standing position and looked for Dana. Tyler was still lying on the ground, mouth wide open, panting. Her dad, like her, had climbed to a standing position. They both converged on Dana, who was buried under Jazz's body. The boy was twitching and, as they approached, lifted onto his elbows, shaking his head as he tried to clear it.

Becca dropped to her knees beside them, her dad reaching out for Jazz on the other side of the prone bodies. Below the young man, Becca saw Dana, the whites showing all the way around her eyes, her dark hair sprayed out on the earth. Closer now, Becca saw that the Hispanic girl wasn't crying; she was laughing.

"You okay?"

Dana looked up at her but with her free arm nudged Jazz. She was laughing again, quietly. She gave Jazz another nudge.

"You're supposed ask my father first, *mi amor.*"

Relief came out in a whoosh as Becca released her pent-up breath.

Jazz, still stunned, was slower on the uptake. It took another second for him to take in his position, with his body pressed tightly against Dana's, her face below his. He blushed furiously and attempted to lift up on his arms to shift his weight off her—which only served to press him even tighter against her, and their legs got tangled.

"Here," said Rob Hawthorne, offering an arm for Jazz to brace against. "Check on Tyler, Becca-bear," he said to his daughter without looking up.

She stood back up, surprised that her equilibrium had returned. Nerve endings jangled under the surge of adrenaline and the urge to run was still there, but she had it under control.

Tyler was sitting, head down between his knees. His right hand rubbed the spot on his chest where Becca's shoulder had caught him. He heard her coming and lifted his head.

"Holy crap," he said. His voice was pitched an octave high and full of disbelief. "What the hell was that?"

"Lightning," she said, hands shaking. "We just missed getting hit by lightning."

"That's a miss?"

"Are we still breathing?"

He gave her a pained look. Raising his face to the clear blue sky above them, he asked, "From where?"

Becca reached down to give Tyler a hand to his feet. She indicated the direction with a nod of her head as he grasped her wrist.

"From over there, I guess."

She leaned back to get leverage and keep the larger boy from pulling her over.

The darkening clouds towered over the peak of the mountain, dominating the sky and moving fast. As they watched, another bolt of lightning slashed toward the ground. Becca waited for the thunder. When it arrived, she did some fast figuring.

"A couple of miles on that one, maybe a bit more." She sought her dad's attention with a subtle motion of her hand. He saw and dipped his head, just a trace of motion.

"Over here," he said. Quickly, the runners assembled around the coach. Dana reached out a hand and brushed some debris off Becca's back. All of them had dirt ground onto their skin, their clothing showing the marks where they had landed. Tyler was still rubbing his chest.

Rob noticed it.

"You okay?"

The boy nodded. "Yeah."

"Good." He looked around at all of them. "We need to get off this mountain and we need to do it quickly. . .." He paused. ". . . but carefully. We can expect a pretty good downpour as soon as that storm gets here, so watch your footing."

Hawthorne filled his lungs and exhaled with an audible sigh. He wore a pained expression, and when he ran a hand down his face, Becca could see his tiredness in the movement.

"Sorry about this." He stretched his shoulders as he drew in another breath. More rumbling echoed down the mountainside and the sun disappeared behind the storm clouds, still towering and increasingly tempestuous. The hard gusts bent the nearby trees, which protested with cracks and pops, the branches flailing at the air.

"Let's get moving. Becca, lead us off. I'll follow up in the rear."

They ordered themselves, Becca in front with Dana behind her, then Tyler and Jazz. She started at an easy pace, feet hardly touching the ground.

"Space out a bit," Rob Hawthorne yelled from the back of the pack. Becca risked a glance behind her and saw that they were jammed in a pack with no time to react. She accelerated for a few strides, giving Dana some room.

As she left the trees of the lake behind, she saw the scree field and rocky pinnacle that she had run past not twenty minutes earlier.

It took a few seconds for her to see the change, and when she did, she went cold inside. Her stomach clenched up, and she worked to quell the shivers that started racing through her limbs.

The outcropping must have taken the brunt of the strike. The tip of it looked different—and the trail that Becca had used was buried under rubble. The ozone smell was overwhelming despite the wind.

Behind her, someone gasped.

"Man, oh man, oh man." Tyler's voice, carried on the wind up to her, was incredulous.

It only took a minute to get to the scree field, and Becca stopped running to pick her way through the rocky stretch at a careful walk. The first fat raindrops speckled the blue-gray granite. A very faint trail was visible, where trail crews had shifted rock to build flatter spots suitable for hiking. The difference was a slender ribbon of firm footing that followed the contour of the scree field. Becca focused on her feet and each step helped with her jangling nerves.

She cleared the field and waited while the others, each in turn, did the same. Dana was breathing hard but holding together.

Tyler was next, muttering under his breath. "Nope, not the hero type. Not me." Becca was sure that he didn't know that his words were carrying. She gave him a reassuring look and Dana laughed, high pitched and a little scared.

"Holy heck, you forgot to tell me that the wild things include the weather."

Jazz came up behind her.

"We'll be okay," he said to her. He looked at Becca and then indicated the outcrop with his eyes. "Chain lightning," he said as the first pelts of rain, fat cold drops, hit them, "reaching ahead of the storm."

"You're bleeding," said Tyler, looking at Becca, his hand making a passing motion toward his own cheek.

Becca reached up and touched her face. A small, hard globule of dried blood stood high on her cheek where the pine needle had punctured her at the lake. As she explored it, a window of awareness opened and she could feel the tenderness in her shoulder from knocking Tyler to the ground, the scuffed palms, the dry mouth. She slammed the window shut, but the sensations floated at the edge of her mind, not quite out of sight.

Becca's dad exited the technical stretch, eyes scanning the hills and clouds. The look of worry still hung on his face but he kept his voice calm.

"Keep it slow, Becca." He didn't have to add any more. Years on the mountains with him had ingrained the lesson. No panicking. Panic killed. Slow down, think. She took the point again and rolled into an easy jog.

The sprinkle changed to a frigid deluge, saturating the trail, the water flowing off the poorly absorbing clay and decomposed granite. Old gullies channeled the water and further eroded the trail. Twice, rocks that looked solid shifted under her feet. Behind her, she could hear the others having the same problem.

She smelled it first when the trail passed around a hummock. Temporarily protected from the battering gusts, the stillness carried an odor, just a whiff. Worry about the storm faded as the new emotion began to nibble at the edge of consciousness. When they cleared the lee of the rock and entered back into the wind it vanished, suppressed by the assault of violent air driving icy water, twin hammers against their mostly exposed skin.

A mile down the trail, the flow of water sluicing over her shoes forced her down to a walk. She looked back and could only see as far as Tyler so she stopped. Dana, bedraggled with her long hair stuck to her head as though it were painted, struggled into sight. Soon the rest appeared. Becca felt like a stick figure dressed in limp nylon shorts chafing on her legs while the skin-tight run top clung even tighter to her torso. All of them wore their clothes stuck to wet skin and all, except for Rob, were shivering. The temperature had dropped at least thirty degrees with the storm.

The wind pummeled them as they stood on a promontory, and Becca saw Dana huddle in the wind shadow that Jazz created. The squall eased off as the fast-moving storm sprinted east away from them.

Becca started out at a walk, still testing the earth below her shoes. As she reached the downturn along the ridge to the forest of dead pines, she caught another whiff and pulled up short. Dana, surprised at the sudden stop, bumped into her.

Below her she could see into the valley, though the valley bottom where the river meandered west to Idaho was hidden by the overhanging cliffs. It was the trees above the river that captured her horrified attention. The dead, beetle-infested trees. Tinder, she thought, as tendrils of smoke lifted from them. One of the strikes had landed in the deadstand, starting a fire that burned hotter than the brief, violent summer storm could quench. The air, scrubbed clean by the rain, allowed her to see the small orange flames licking at the wood.

The others gathered around her as the flames, driven by the wind, leapt to the copse of dead pines. A lodgepole pine next to the trail ignited. Long dead and thoroughly dry, the ends of the branches were first to catch, the flame flowing from the tip to the trunk as though coated in gasoline. The tree erupted into a giant pyre. Seconds later, it exploded with a echoing boom, sending sparks of new fire deeper into the stand and over the edge of the cliff toward the unseen river.

Rob was standing next to his daughter as they all watched the consuming fire obliterate their path. She heard him snort, not in anger or astonishment, but disbelief.

"Son of a gun!" His voice was low but emphatic.

She stared at her dad, they all did, waiting for him to tell them what they were going to do, but he stood stock-still, staring.

Becca's breath caught in her throat and something gripped her, powerful and mean. She wrapped her arms around herself.

She tried to stop her hands from shaking but the effort at control just transferred the reaction to the rest of her. Her stomach wrenched tighter, the tightness spread into her chest, and a new sensation overtook Becca.

Fear.

Chapter 9

Rob reached into his pack, snatching the radio out and hitting the On button almost in one motion. Becca heard the static, spikes of white noise as the now-distant lightning interfered with the signal.

"Jim, you got a copy?" he said, a forced calm applied to his words. The others closed in on the radio, listening for a response. The speaker crackled and spat but through the noisy reception, they heard Eagle respond. The signal was garbled but some of the words came through clear enough to be understood.

"... *okay, heading for ... fire ...*" And then the voice faded.

Rob keyed the mike. "Jim, everybody is okay up here. Fire has cut off the trail." He let go of the Transmit button but either Eagle couldn't hear him or the signals were getting lost in the atmosphere. He tried again.

"Fire on the trail, Jim. Need another route."

This time there was a crackle and their straining ears picked up a single word: "... *lake* ..." and the signal was lost again.

"Repeat, Jim."

But the speaker emitted a steady stream of static.

Below them, a quarter of the trees were already lit and the fire was licking sideways into the healthy trees, hungry for more fuel. The green trees were slower to light but one, nearest the hottest part of the fire, exploded as the internal pressures and outside temperatures went wildly out of balance. The sound reached them on a short delay. The wind fanned the shower of sparks into more dry underbrush and new flames flickered and fed on the kindling. The smell of the smoke was strong and growing as the flames encroached up the mountain. Rob gave up on the radio.

"Back to the lake," he said, pointing to the muddy mess they had just traversed. "Walk." He looked at the scared faces and Becca watched him smile. "Now, people."

Dana pulled even with Becca as they scurried back uphill. "What are we going to do?" Her words flooded out in a rush, breathy and jerky.

"For now, keep moving," said Becca. She fought to keep her voice reassuring. "We'll figure it out when we get to the lake."

The rain disappeared as quickly as it had drenched them and, in the resurgence of summer heat, the rocks sent thin trails of vaporous steam twisting up from the fast-drying surfaces. The sky above hung gray and heavy; the mountaintops were shrouded in damp fog, the steam from the evaporating rain mixing with the smoke.

In the heavy silence, they kept moving while he sounds of new trees igniting harassed them, an occasional boom to punctuate the death of another tree. The stench of the scorched wood permeated the air around them.

Becca slipped, recovered by putting a hand down, and wiped the muddy palm on her shorts as she came back upright.

"You okay?"

Becca glanced over to Dana and saw the apprehension the other girl covered up with her concern for Becca. Becca reached out with her clean hand and put it on Dana's shoulder, giving her a squeeze.

"It's okay." As she said it, thirst intruded, and she reached for her water bottle.

"Has it been thirty minutes?" asked Dana. She was breathing hard from exertion and emotion; so was everyone else.

Becca gave a short, sharp laugh, full of tension. "Hell if I know. Does it make much difference?" To her own ears, she sounded shrill, but she managed a grim smile.

"Good job, ladies," said Rob from just behind them. His words were measured. "Just keep moving."

Becca looked over her shoulder. Her father walked with mechanical precision, arms locked in a ninety-degree angle, and kept his eyes up the hill.

Just like he was racing, thought Becca, turning forward again. Her own movement was sloppier so she tightened up. As she did, the effort level dropped slightly. Dana noticed and matched her as they used short but powerful strides to climb.

They reached the lake, and Becca took another long drink. Tyler watched her and nudged Jazz in the ribs as he did the same. While Rob fumbled in his pack, the kids wordlessly drained their bottles and walked to the lake for a refill. Smoke was filling the bowl formed around the lake, sitting low on the water like fog, the smell recalling past campfires of camping trips with her dad.

"I forgot to pack marshmallows. . . ."

Becca thought she had kept the words to herself, but Dana gave her an incredulous look, and Jazz smiled.

When they returned, Rob stood facing down-trail, a topo map spread out between his hands. The baggie he used to protect the map from weather was hanging from a corner of his mouth while he squinted at the fine lines to locate their position. Finding it, he folded the map over to focus on the quadrant with the lake. He looked around and sighed.

"Folks, we got a problem." He dropped the map a bit. "I don't see another trail coming up here. There is one that keeps heading up toward the peaks but I don't see much sense in moving farther from rescue. The other option is to stay here and take our chances."

"What if the fire gets up to these trees?" said Tyler.

Becca was shaking her head.

Tyler looked resentful. "It's a fair question," he said.

Rob looked to his daughter and then answered Tyler. "We can get into the lake. It's not the fire I'm worried about." He sighed again. "Most people in a fire don't die from flame; they die from asphyxiation from the smoke."

Tyler blanched and Dana looked nauseous. Jazz kept looking at Rob steadily, waiting for a plan.

Becca kept her voice low as she peeked around her dad's shoulder at the map. "Hypothermia. We're wet, and the temperatures are going to drop with nightfall."

"We can cuddle up like puppies and share heat," said Rob. "We'll probably be okay on that score."

Becca saw the expressions on the boys' faces and knew that her own face and Dana's shared it. With only run gear on, cuddling with Jazz and Tyler was much more intimate than she ever intended to be with either of them.

"We can use the pine needles and stuff to help," Jazz said, having the grace to look embarrassed.

Something on the map captured her eye, and a small voice whispered to her. *"It's an old trail. . . ."*

Her father spoke. "We need to be ready to move the second help gets here. If the fire hops the open space—and I don't want to lie to you, it probably will—we'll retreat. We can't go up the mountain too much farther without climbing gear and much warmer clothes. We only go into the lake if the heat gets overwhelming."

Becca leaned against her dad, standing on her tiptoes and looking over his shoulder as a sliver of hope cut a shaft through her gloom.

"Dad," she said as she reached around him for the map. He staggered a bit from the contact, half-turning to reduce the pressure. As he did, the map moved back out of her reach.

"I need the map," she said. Her words carried an undercurrent of excitement and she grasped again, this time catching a corner. Rob frowned but let go.

"I looked, Becca," he said, "there aren't any other trails."

She ignored him and unfolded the map out to its full size. Her father had trimmed off the edges of the map to save weight and space but the closer she looked, the more certain she was that this was the same topo that Eagle had at the lodge in the camp.

Her eyes traced the trail up to the lake and saw the steep path they had just run. Eagle's voice came back to her.

"This was a longer route, but easier for women and children to climb to this lake. . . ." She could see his finger tapping the map on the wall.

She looked up from the map and stared at her dad. "We can get off the mountain."

He shook his head. "We'll never make it through the smoke. I'm not going to take that chance with you guys."

"We can't stay here." Everybody stared at her and Becca's scalp tingled as she fought to keep her voice steady. "If this is the same map that was at camp, there's another trail"—she tried to point at it but the limp map fell over as soon as she released an edge—"that Uncle Jim has been restoring."

"*Uncle* Jim?" muttered Dana, perplexed.

Becca ignored her, bending to the ground to smooth out the topo. "He had this map—not *this* map but the same quad—on the wall and it had a big red line running from here." She traced out the rough route down to the river trail.

Her dad frowned as he studied the squiggly lines. The trail that Becca outlined passed directly through the densest part of the forest but was over the ridge and partially protected.

"Dad," Becca's voice was insistent, "we can at least look for it."

He looked up at the faces around him and then at his daughter kneeling in the dirt, her eyes pleading.

"How sure are you?" he asked, eyes narrowed.

Becca hesitated, then raised her chin stubbornly even as her stomach dropped.

"Positive."

He nodded once decisively and stood up.

"Let's find that trail then."

Chapter 10

They wore new scratches and a gritty layer of sweat by the time they reached the other end of the lake. The pristine water lapped against rock as the runners resorted to forcing their way through the undergrowth when the scant rock shoreline disappeared under thick brush. The low vegetation, spiky more often than leafy, grabbed and snagged clothing and left slender red threads of blood on their legs and arms.

The farther around the lake they struggled, the more anxious Becca became. She peered into the wooded hillside hoping for a hint of an opening. Nothing presented itself and the smoke was getting thicker. The trail had to be here; it looped around the fire, out of the danger zone, out of the smoke.

Beside her father, Tyler coughed, a phlegmy expulsion of air that startled a Steller's jay into flight. The flash of blue sped off, darting up and pivoting around a tall stand of trees, and was gone. Becca traced its flight as it passed over Jazz, who was staring at his feet in the soft mud of the shore. Dana stood close to him as she had the entire bushwhack around the lake.

He looked up and saw her staring at him.

"Go a little that way!" He waved an arm to get her to turn to her left.

"Why?" she shouted back.

He didn't answer but just gestured emphatically while he slowly walked forward to the first tree, head bent.

Tyler closed the gap to her. "We might as well." He hunched over as he hacked again.

Becca's eyes were starting to water and burn so she wiped them quickly. She stepped over a rotting log, dodging the jagged remains of branches that threatened to tear more skin, and entered the deeper gloom under the canopy.

"More," came Jazz's insistent voice.

"Sometimes that boy pisses me off," said Tyler. He pushed past a thick branch and held it so it would not snap back and slap Becca.

"Oh good," said Becca. "I thought maybe it was just me." She stepped past him into a narrow glade. She cocked her head to one side and wiped her eyes again to be sure.

"Dude, you see that?" she asked Tyler, hope building.

"No way," said Tyler, shaking his head.

Running the length of the glade was a faint and twisty gap in the brush, less a trail than an absence of overgrowth. Becca walked toward it, keeping her eyes focused on the spot. Beneath her feet she sensed the change, a smoothing of the earth, and she looked down.

Deer tracks embedded in the damp soil pointed like arrows toward the lake, interspersed with pellets, probably from a doe and fawns, from the size of the prints.. She ran her gaze over the ground and picked out more tracks, following the general outline she had seen at the edge of the clearing.

Jazz was yelling again, sounding agitated, but his words were lost in the thin air and among the thick boles of the trees.

Becca looked back. The only person in sight was Tyler. Her father had diverted to Jazz to find out why the boy was yelling.

"Over here!" she shouted.

Tyler looked stubborn. "That's not a trail."

"It better be," she said. "How many times are you going to hack up a lung before you get it? By the time the fire gets here, we'll already be toast."

The freckles stood out on Tyler's face as he stubbornly shook his head. "The camp knows we're up here. They'll send some help."

"From where?" Becca couldn't help it—her sarcasm mocked his naïveté. "How are they going to get up here when we can't even get out? Unicorns?"

"Maybe a helicopter can—"

"TYLER!"

He looked surprised and a little hurt at the glare she gave him, but he acquiesced without another argument. Head down, either trying to keep an eye on the trail or because his feelings were bruised, he walked back toward Jazz.

As he slipped out of sight, Becca turned back to the game trail. She tried to plot it in her mind in relation to the line she remembered from the map. It was about the right spot, she decided, but worry gnawed at her. Calling it a trail was generous.

As she waited, her eyes drifted, focusing on a tree a hundred yards distant. It dawned on her that she was staring at a triangular blaze painted onto the tree, all three side equal in length. Heart thumping with excitement, she began jogging along the path to the tree, eyes fixed on the mark as sinuous branches clutched at her ankles.

The blaze was about six feet up on the tree and about three inches to a side. The paint coated the outer layer of the bark. She reached up, touching the rough edge of the bark. The mark didn't penetrate into the crannies of the bark. The pigment was clean and intact; it hadn't been subjected to the brutal winters of the high mountains yet.

Uncle Jim didn't clear the whole trail, she thought, *but he marked it.* A shiver of excitement went through her as she tried to visualize the rest of the trail, the red line stretching to the river below etched in her memory.

She turned as the group caught up with her. Dana wore pieces of twigs and needles in her hair and had a long cut on her arm that was seeping a slow dribble of blood.

Becca glanced at the arm as her dad glanced past her to inspect the trail marking.

"Good eyes," he said. His voice was flat as he continued. "Everybody drink up. Once we start rolling, we don't stop until we get to the river."

She didn't look up as she rummaged in her fanny pack. "Jazz figured it out." She glanced up at him.

Jazz shrugged. "There were a lot of deer tracks," he said. "I just figured they'd follow the easiest path to get a drink."

Becca opened her first-aid kit, fishing out a large gauze pad. "We don't have time, Becca."

"Here," she said, ignoring her dad and handing it to Dana. "Press this against that cut and hold it while I put some tape on it."

Dana cast her eyes down to the gauze, and then snuck a glance at Becca's dad. He waved.

"Make it quick."

Dana glanced at her arm. There were two rivulets of bright red curling down to her fingers.

"Jeez, I didn't think it was that bad."

Becca worked fast, spreading some ointment on the cuts and wrapping adhesive tape around Dana's forearm. In less than sixty seconds, she was done and putting the kit back into her pack. She didn't look at her dad.

Hawthorne was squinting as he canvassed the nearby trees. It took Becca a second to acknowledge that her dad couldn't see the flashes at a distance. Seconds later, she pointed to a tree barely visible through the leaves and low-hanging limbs.

"Over there, I think," said Becca.

"We don't have time for '*I think*,' " said Hawthorne. "Is it or isn't it?"

Becca stiffened, and she snapped her mouth open to defend herself, but Jazz confirmed it for her.

"She's right," he said. "I can see it, too."

Hawthorne turned to face the boy. "Lead us off."

They went in single file, Jazz stumbling as he tried to pick the easiest route only to discover deadfall covered in new growth blocking the way. Twice, they diverted around.

The undergrowth was thicker around the new waypoint and the remnants of the trail vanished into a sea of green. A pall of gray air infiltrated the woods, filling the spaces between boughs. Becca squinted as she scanned the direction they faced. Nothing. As she shifted her field of vision, she spotted the next mark, off to the right.

"There!" Her voice was sounding raspy and, behind her, Tyler hacked.

Jazz took the front position again, bulling through the unyielding vegetation. Three more times they found the triangle marks in trees. Becca estimated that they had covered nearly a half a mile, but it had taken them fifteen minutes of frenetic effort.

Too slow, she thought, as she searched for the next mark. The acrid smoke rolled in toward them and, for the first time, she could hear a noise, like a roaring hiss except it was far in the distance. The hiss added pops and more dull booms, and in her mind, she could see the flames ravaging the trees below them as it hunted fresh food up the mountain.

"Not far enough," she murmured. Dana swung around to look at her. The other girl's eyes were red-rimmed from the smoke, and Dana blinked a lot to keep them moist. Becca nodded to reassure her. She looked up to her dad, needing some reassurance of her own, but he was focused on Jazz's back, following the path the larger teen forged while snapping thin branches, widening the trail for the girls and Tyler.

Jazz, breathing heavily, reached the next white triangle and leaned on the tree, rivulets of sweat streaming down his face. His legs and arms were crisscrossed with scratches, but his expression, grimly focused, showed no indication that he felt them.

They grouped up again around the tree, and Becca struggled to find the next mark. The smoke continued its steady infiltration. She shook her head in frustration as she listened to the others gasping, more from emotion than exertion, except for Jazz.

"Which way, Becca?" asked her father. He was staring at her intently, but his voice was soft.

Her eyes darted, looking over his shoulder, past Jazz and the marked tree. She turned back to face her dad, a hollowness spreading through her body. There was nothing to see, not a hint. Only trees and brush, the scent of the forest, the smell of the fire. The air tasted like bitter burned sap and her face scrunched as she made one last visual circuit. She turned to face the group, eyes wide.

"I don't know!"

Chapter 11

The forest never really got quiet, never perfectly still. She learned that when she was a little girl, camping with her dad, sleepless the first time in the tent as a parade of nighttime animals moved past. Even the wind would whisper and the trees would answer. Around her now, though, she could hear the forest awakening to danger. These were new sounds, more urgent, as the birds, the early warning system of the forest, fled above them, headed east.

"Okay," said her dad. The same quiet voice, acknowledging that they missed a turn—or that there weren't any more turns, that Jim Eagle hadn't marked any more of the trail.

Another shiver hit Becca, and she could see her fears mirrored in Dana's eyes.

"So we go back?" said Tyler.

Rob Hawthorne shook his head. "We can't." He cut off Tyler with another shake of his head as the boy started to object.

"We're committed. The smoke is getting too dense to see and we don't have flashes to follow on going this way."

Becca looked back the way they had come. A leafy wall of green foliage and gray smoke drifted behind them. The sound of the burning forest crackled in the distance, slowly getting louder. With a start, she heard her dad talking to her again.

"Becca, how far can you see?"

"About twenty yards." Her voice surprised her. Hoarse from the grimy air and running, it sounded detached and calm, though she could taste the smoke. The empty feeling was still there, lurking, but her voice exerted control over it.

Rob was nodding.

"That might work." He looked at Jazz. "How about you?"

"Not quite as far," Jazz admitted.

Rob dug into his run pack. "Becca, get out your rope."

Becca swung the bag around from her back to the front and unzipped it. Beside her, Dana did the same. They both pulled out thirty-foot lengths at the same time. Jazz was slower. Only Tyler didn't have any rope.

"Okay, here's the plan. I'm going to anchor this end of a ladder. Each of you will have a loop of rope in either hand and be a rung. Becca will be at the other end, unless someone thinks they can see better in this crap than she can." As he talked, he started to put bowline knots on the ends of his rope, creating loops that wouldn't slip. Becca quickly tied hers to match Rob's.

Dana and Tyler shook their heads.

"Not me," said Dana. "I can't see anything except trees and smoke." She fumbled, trying to emulate Becca and Rob.

"Here," said Jazz, extending his arms out and demonstrating slowly, first making a loop a foot up the rope, then passing the free end through the loop, under the backside of the extended end, and back through the loop, snugging it tight. "Like that."

She copied him on each move and ended up with a passable knot. She looked up and her dark eyes met his.

"Thanks."

He nodded.

Tyler snorted and turned to Rob.

"So what are we doing?"

Rob gave him a steady look and, when he resumed speaking, maintained the same calm voice.

"We're going to put Becca out as far as we can and get her to spot the next mark. It's too smoky to just wander off—the chance of getting separated is too big—so we're tying everybody together."

"What if she doesn't see anything?" Tyler's jaw was set hard and his words carried an undercurrent of anger.

"We don't borrow trouble until we have to," said Rob. Looking at the surrounding forest, he continued, "Becca goes out first, then Jazz, you, and last is Dana. Shout to the next person in the line to pass messages. We'll all probably be able to hear it but let's keep it clean and clear. Got it?"

Tyler shrugged as Dana and Jazz murmured affirmatives. Becca looked along the line they'd traveled to get to this tree and eased out on a course as straight as she could manage, holding on to the rope. Jazz held the other end.

The rope caught and tugged on the branches, so she lifted it above her head until she felt it go tight.

"Anything, Becca?" her dad called out behind her.

She looked left to right, eyes darting from tree to tree looking for the next marker, but nothing materialized. Taking action calmed her, she discovered.

"No," she yelled back.

The rope in her hand slackened as Jazz advanced on her. She waited until he joined her before advancing again. Nothing, and

83

the sequence repeated itself. In the distance, she heard Tyler coughing. Again nothing. She squinted, looking forward, the smoke much denser ahead. Jazz came up, the lines of sweat on his face stained black at the edges from soot.

"I can't see crap," he said.

She shrugged. "Maybe this next one," she said, but she didn't meet his eyes.

She could feel wind on her face, driving the smoke at her as she left Jazz. She was nearly at the end of the rope when she slipped. Becca turned sideways to recover her balance, her leg extended as she leaned into the uphill leg.

A canyon, she thought, and Eagle's words floated back to her. *". . . easier for women and children to climb . . ."* With a flash of insight, she clambered back up the slope. They wouldn't have been climbing the steep canyon walls; they would have followed a shallower course.

"We're headed the wrong way," she shouted at Jazz and walked through the undergrowth toward him.

He relayed the information back to the others and waited until she caught up before heading toward Tyler. Quickly, they reassembled around Rob.

"There's a canyon," explained Becca to her dad. "If we keep going in a straight line, we fall right into it."

Rob considered the new information and looked to one side. "That way, you think?" he asked.

Becca started to answer *I think so* but hesitated. She broke eye contact with him by closing her eyes. In her mind, she called up an image of the red line on the green map. Eyes still closed, she lifted her right arm up to point in the direction they were going. She took a steadying breath and, tracing the map, lifted her left arm to point to a spot sixty degrees from their angle of travel.

She opened her eyes and said, "That way." She pushed past a thicket of shrubby cinquefoil, the bright flowers scattering petals at her feet as she escaped to the semi-clear space on the other side.

They repeated the cycle, Jazz following, waiting for Tyler to join him, Tyler waiting for Dana. Becca maneuvered through the ghostly trees, looking for the next white triangle. She inspected each tree, looking from the foot to the lowest branches, much taller than Eagle would have been able to reach, but couldn't see a sign that the Nez Perce had been here.

She looked back at Jazz. He was watching her, waiting, hoping for a sign, but his face looked grim. He jerked his chin up, meeting her eyes. She nodded and turned back to search as though the trees would suddenly yield the secret way, but they stood mute, awaiting their fate as the smoke thickened and the roar of the flames grew. Becca shuddered and impulsively slipped the loop end of the rope around the nearest bush.

"Becca!"

She ignored Jazz as she locked her eyes on a tree ten yards in front of her. As she moved, she scuffed her shoes along the ground, leaving gouges in the loose topsoil. She dragged a toe around the base of the tree, and with her back tight against the bark of the tree, lined up the next target.

Becca heard Jazz hollering down the line, but the responses were muted and distant and she kept her eyes forward as she scuffed ahead.

With her eyes up, she almost missed it except for the feel under her feet, a change in texture that alerted something deep inside her and made her stop. She looked at her feet but couldn't discern what had caused her to halt. At the edge of her vision, a small boulder, maybe a foot in diameter, with a line where it had sat in the dirt, leaned against the tree she was aiming for. The dirty bottom faced her.

Dirt.

She looked at her feet again, and this time saw the marks of a shovel, nearly washed away by the rain, where the soil was tamped down to fill in the hole left when the rock was rolled out. To her left, branches, the ends still white and fleshy, recently cut.

"Over here," she said in a loud voice, trying to maintain her calm.

No response from Jazz, so she shouted again.

This time, she didn't care that her voice wasn't calm.

She was standing on the end of the trail. To her left, less than ten yards away, was open running room, their escape around the fire and down to the river.

Chapter 12

Her dad was the first to appear through the gloom, holding his end of the line. It took Becca by surprise. She expected Jazz to materialize. A second later, in a flash of insight, she understood that he had pivoted the entire line around Jazz to reach her. Even if she came up with nothing, they still had the ability to go back the way they had come. But only partway, she reminded herself. They were committed when they lost track of the trail marks.

Inwardly, she wished that someone else had joined him.

As her father came toward her, she waited for him to yell at her for leaving the safety line and freelancing. Instead, he gave her a rare smile and an odd expression that she couldn't figure out.

"Hello, Becca," he said, over the popcorn sounds and the constant roar of the wall of fire closing on them, closer than ever. The blowing smoke made the forest around them a surrealistic world of thinly upright columns supporting a roof of nebulous gray clouds, and the short sightlines denied them any sort of perspective. It was a cocoon that they needed to break out of to reach clean, clear sunlight.

He glanced down the trail and nodded his head, small satisfied movements, and then looked at her again.

"Very nice job." Another smile, wider this time. "I was thinking that it might be time to panic after all."

Nothing gets to him, thought Becca, slightly shocked at the humor but mostly relieved that he hadn't yelled.

She took a deep breath that ended in a coughing fit, and he gripped her shoulder.

"Easy."

Dana was next, followed by Tyler, and finally Jazz. Becca winced when she saw the mass of cuts on the boy's powerful thighs and along the bony sides of his forearms. Each runner checked the trail as they joined the group, evaluating the runnability of the surface. It was narrow, barely as wide as their hips, but the footing was clear of most obstacles. They could make speed.

"How's everybody doing?" asked Rob. Jazz shrugged and Tyler tried to look hostile but managed only to look frightened. Dana stood close to Jazz.

"Lead us out, Becca. Keep it slow," said Rob, turning to her. To the others, he said, "Tyler, behind her, then Dana, and Jazz. I get the caboose."

Becca hesitated, waiting for more directions, and her father made a scooting motion with his hands, so she unplanted herself from the spot by the overturned rock and headed down-trail toward the river.

Pine needles covered the trail except where Eagle had scraped them away to improve the footing, banking some turns, filling in hollows, and removing awkwardly placed rubble. Even without the groove worn in by steady traffic that developed trails exhibited, enough construction, in balance with the natural terrain, had made the trail plainly visible even in the poor lighting. The paint markings on the boles of the evergreens reappeared as well, periodic reassurances resolving themselves in the haze, confirming that the course she steered headed in the correct direction.

They were headed downhill, not steeply but steadily, and, as she ran, the part of her mind obsessing on the noise from the conflagration noted that it was moving behind them as they curved around the perimeter of the burn. She stumbled slightly on a tree root partially hidden by low vegetation but regained her balance with minimal effort.

Focus, she thought, and settled into an easy rhythm. Eagle had crafted well and a touch of regret filled her that she had to run his path in desperation instead of joy. She banked through a turn onto another straightaway, feet moving quickly and surely, feeling the earth. Each stride brought her closer to the river, closer to—

"Hey," shouted a hoarse Tyler behind her, "you're killing us."

Surprised, Becca leaned back, shortening her stride as she did, to slow down. She glanced over her shoulder and saw Tyler, barely in sight. She drifted to a stop and waited. Tyler caught up, face gray and grimacing. His breaths were heaving and unsteady and, as Becca watched, he dug out a red-cased inhaler. He shook the vial of medication vigorously before putting it to his mouth, taking a deep, wet breath, and pressing down on the tube to propel the aerosol into his lungs.

"Asthma?" guessed Becca as Dana appeared and joined them. Jazz was right behind her and Rob ran close on the taller boy's heels.

"Yeah," said Tyler. "It's why I gave up smoking." He was shaking his head self-deprecatingly as he spoke but managed a grim smile.

"You okay, dude?" asked Jazz.

Tyler's reply was interrupted by the sharp cracks of broken limbs coming toward them up the hill. They all turned in time to see a black bear emerge. Richly cinnamon colored, he stopped on the trail, stood upright with paws raised, and stared at them in surprise, mutually felt. From a distance of forty feet, the intelligence in the liquid brown eyes shone. The bear woofed, softly, and it scented the air, nostrils flaring and rounded ears twitching.

Becca held her breath.

Deciding they posed no immediate threat, the animal lowered itself and, with a startling amount of speed, reentered the forest, snapping a downed sapling like a popsicle stick as it passed out of sight.

"Can I borrow your knife?" asked Dana, standing next to her. Her voice, like everyone else's, reminded Becca of a lifelong smoker, but there was also humor built into it, and when Becca looked at the other girl, she saw awe.

"Sure."

"It won't help you," said Jazz, frowning. "That bear had to be at least four hundred pounds."

Dana chuckled and reached out to pat him on the shoulder. To Becca, she said, "He's very cute and so sincere, I think I'll keep him."

Jazz looked confused and oddly happy, but Rob broke in.

"People, let's keep moving."

As Becca started to walk away, shifting to a jog, she heard Tyler speaking to Jazz.

"Dude, you're doomed."

Jazz's answer was lost as she accelerated away.

Fresh air.

That was Becca's clue that they had passed the edge of the fire, a welcome gust of clean air swirling the noxious fumes away, giving her a glimpse ahead. They were at the base of the ridge now, dropping through a grove of cedars, and the trail got steeper as it descended to a tributary of the river. The views snatched between the trees showed a swollen creek, brown muddy water rushing forward, eroding the banks as it surged with rain runoff. On her mental map, Becca saw the creek between them and the river trail. They were going to get wet. *Wetter,* she thought. Her clothes were still damp from the brief, intense rain and the sweat of their race to the river.

The footing was soft and semi-dry. Eons of accumulation of twigs and needles left the color of the trail a reddish brown in the dim light. As they got close to the feeder creek, the noisy rush of the water covered the sounds of their feet. Several times Becca had glanced over her shoulder to reassure herself that the others were still behind her.

An occasional rumble of distant thunder rolled off the peaks above them and around the valley, a reminder to hurry.

The creek widened as it approached the river and Becca exited the end of the trail at a clearing overlooking the confluence. The clearing sat on a shelf six feet above the dirty waters and the creek was only sixteen or eighteen feet across. Becca's eyes grew as she measured the velocity of the storm-driven flow, a piece of flotsam ripping past, dipping and rising on the waves.

"Damn it!" Her teeth were clenched so hard it hurt as she scowled from the bank. She stared at the powerful currents, narrowed eyes glancing to the opposite bank, looking for a calm stretch of water. *It's not fair,* she thought—and grimaced because she already knew her dad's reply. *Life's not fair. Deal.*

"What?" asked Tyler, cruising to a stop behind her. He looked beyond her and said, "We're crossing that *how?*"

Becca threw up her hands and turned away without answering. Her dad and the other two runners came into the flat. Dana looked tired. Becca did a fast calculation and figured they had covered nearly eleven miles. She could feel some achiness in her legs but she was a high-mileage runner and knew it would fade.

"How many miles do you run, Dana?" she asked the other girl. Her dad gave her a fast, perceptive look before focusing his attention on the barrier in front of them.

Dana glanced at her and smiled weakly. "About three or five a day. Maybe thirty per week with a long run." She cocked her head to the left and thought. "I think this might be my longest run ever."

Jazz stood close to Dana. Despite the multitude of abrasions, he radiated strength and grit. As she spoke, his face transformed and he flashed a warm smile at Dana. "Congratulations on the PR."

"I think we can ford the creek," said Rob, breaking into the moment. "First, we need to get a safety line across. " He walked away from the edge and dug out his piece of rope. The others did the same and he quickly fashioned them into a longer length. He tested the knots by tying one of the free ends to a tree and having all three boys play tug-of-war. The knots held.

Hawthorne undid the rope at the tree and walked with it to the bank.

"Jazz, Tyler," he said, glancing at each in turn, "you guys anchor the rope on this end while I cross." He walked in the opposite direction of the water flow.

"I'm going to walk on a diagonal to the flow and cut some of the pressure, so it's going to be kind of an arc." He made eye contact with the boys again and smiled wryly. "If I go down, I'd appreciate it if you'd start pulling like heck."

Seeing agreement, he attached the rope around his waist.

Twenty yards up, he started the slippery descent to the creek. His feet splashed into the water and he waited a moment, seeking his balance and getting a feel for the current.

"WANT SOME HELP?"

Becca jerked her head up and around to the source of the shouted words.

She saw Jim Eagle standing on the opposite bank with a confident grin, relaxed and ready.

Chapter 13

The Bridger coach stood near the edge of the embankment on his side of the water, an acute triangle of land, the supplement to the wider expanse on their side. The creek joined the river at an angle and the tip of Eagle's side was accentuated by an old log, grayed with the thick base of the trunk embedded into the sand as it pointed down the river like a signpost to the inevitable.

"Glad to see you, partner," hollered Rob, shifting out of the water, setting his feet squarely in the loose dirt. "Where are the kids?"

"Safe with Joseph."

Becca's brow creased as she tried to make sense of Joseph with the other runners, since he was supposed to be at camp. His words, *"be careful,"* sounded eerily prophetic now. Becca shrugged and focused on crossing the river, checking out the current. Beside her, the boys and Dana were quiet, waiting for the coaches to figure out how to ford the fast-flowing creek.

Eagle's face was almost as sooty as theirs and streaks of sweat had left trails along his temples and cheeks. He stood nonchalantly, but the intensity of the fire in his eyes betrayed the tension inside him. Eagle paused while he gauged the situation. "I think the current's too strong to just walk it, Rob."

"I figured it might take a try or two."

"Yeah, or they might find your body in Portland after the river dumps you out."

As Eagle spoke, Rob clambered back up the slope, the soft earth sloughing away under his feet as he pushed up to the top, dragging himself up the last two feet hand-over-hand using a convenient bush. Stable, but caked in mud, he walked back until he stood with the group.

"Got a plan?"

"Let's get the rope over first. You got enough to tie off on that end and have a safety harness?"

It was Rob's turn to gauge the gulf. The clearings on either side didn't have decent points to secure the line. They'd have to stretch to the trees and leave some slack in the line to reach the water.

"No. We got enough to get across but probably not enough to do it twice for the safety rig."

"That'll have to do."

As they spoke, Rob took a baseball-sized rock and wrapped the free end of rope around it, tying it off loosely with a slip knot before starting the second loop, perpendicular to the first. He cinched the line tight and hefted it. The rock slipped slightly and he adjusted the tension again.

Above, Becca heard the buzz of an aircraft, but the foliage was too dense to see the sky except in glimpses in the cleft over the water. Her dad heard the plane at the same time Becca did and glanced up. *Spotter plane,* she figured, *scoping out the fire,* and put it out of her mind.

Rob refocused on the work in front of him. When he was satisfied with the balance of the weight, he bounced the rock in his hand.

"Ready?" he shouted over to Eagle.

"Anytime," came the dry response.

Rob cocked his right arm and, stepping out with his left leg, hurled the rock toward Eagle. A splash greeted his efforts as the trajectory of the rock landed it in the creek. Rob snorted and carefully dragged the rock back, making sure that he didn't knock the loops off.

Twice more he tried, and the last time the rock hit the base of the embankment before falling in the water.

"This is why you were a runner, huh?" shouted Eagle with a smirk, crinkles at the corners of his eyes.

Rob muttered something as he tugged on the line again. As he pulled the dripping weight up again, Tyler stepped up next to him.

"Hey, Coach, can I see that for a second?"

Rob turned with the rock in his hand. Before he had a chance to reply, Tyler snatched the stone from his hand, pivoted, and fired a fastball screaming at Eagle's midsection. Eagle leapt out of the way and the rock hit a tree with a solid *thunk!* that left a gouge in the bark. The safety line trailed out to the bank.

"Can we go now?" Tyler deadpanned.

Eagle loosened the knots on his end. Quickly, he wound the rope around the girth of a tree. Jazz released slack on his side to drop the rope toward the fast-flowing surface.

"That's good, bud," said Eagle. Jazz cinched the rope, testing it by leaning in with all his strength. It didn't budge.

The two coaches began shouting back and forth, deciding on how to make the crossing.

Becca watched the proceedings but judiciously stayed out of the way. An idea grew as Jazz suspended himself on the rope, not content with the first test.

"Still got that rope?" she asked Dana.

Dana nodded, looking at Becca with questioning eyes, while reaching into her pack and pulling it out. As Dana dug into her pack, Becca foraged in hers, coming up with the knife. She slipped it open, the blade locking against the catch, the four-inches of sharpened steel gleaming.

"Measure out about—" Becca hesitated, squinting. "—about three feet."

Dana slid her hands until she reached the designated length.

"Okay, let's cut it here." Becca made a loop, and placed the knife inside it. The sharp edge quickly sawed through the casing and interior cord. She handed the knife to Dana.

"You cut the rest, just like that," she said. "One for everybody."

She strode to the line and, with Jazz watching, tied a bowline knot around it, making a loop with enough slack that it could slide freely. She added another loop, creating a handhold.

Jazz raised an eyebrow in grudging respect, then his gaze reverted to Dana.

"Cut away from you!"

Dana stood with the rope doubled in her left hand, pulling up on the blade with her right. She blushed, reversed her grip on the handle and, curling her wrists down, followed his directions.

When they were done, they moved the loops down to the edge where Rob had stomped steps into the embankment to limit the chance for falling. He glanced up and nodded.

"Smart," he said, looking at Jazz. Before Jazz could correct him, Hawthorne started organizing them for the crossing.

"Tyler, you're headed over first. Coach Eagle will meet you and help you up the side. Once you get there, help anchor the rope, keep the side-to-side movement down. Got it?"

The freckled youth bobbed his head and twined the hand grip over his wrist and grasped the knot. He climbed down and stepped into the water.

"Crap, that's cold!" he shouted, and stepped deeper.

"Turn at an angle, Tyler," said Hawthorne, stationed with his feet in the water as Jazz stabilized the rope above. "And baby steps."

Tyler complied, scuffling along. The currents, unpredictable, buffeted him, and Becca could see the flex in his bicep as he hauled on the wrist rope to maintain balance. Eagle hauled him out of the water when he reached the far side and practically pushed him up the bank.

"Dana, you're next."

"I liked the rope bridge better," she said as she left Becca's side. Silently, Becca agreed.

Her traverse was harder than Tyler's and she moved slower. She kept a death grip on the looped rope in her left hand and reached across her body to keep her right hand on the guide. Twice she paused, her unseen foot seeking a firm spot to land. Eagle angled out and grasped her by the arm, almost dragging her ashore.

"Becca, you're up."

Becca drew a deep breath and climbed down to her father. He gave her a reassuring smile.

"Nice and easy."

She glanced his way without really seeing him. Like the runners that went first, she used her left hand to latch on to the loops she had made. Her eyes on the guide rope, she stepped into the creek. Prickles of goose bumps appeared on her legs immediately and tremors in her thighs made her tremble. She slipped out into deeper water. When she looked down, it was all brown and murky and roiled; she couldn't see a thing. Carefully, she moved her right foot, found a rock, and set her weight on it. She moved her left foot until she stood with her slender hips turned sideways, letting water sweep by. She sent the right foot out and repeated the sequence. After every pair of steps, she stopped, caught a breath, and then moved again.

The water clung and snapped at her shorts when the depth crossed the top of her legs. Her left leg wavered below her when she took her next step and she flexed a bit more at the knee. Even through the soles of her shoes, she could feel the slime on the rounded rubble that lined the creek.

She paused again . . . deep breath, and she shook out the tension in her shoulders and briefly relaxed her grips on the ropes. Another deep breath and she moved.

The rock under her left foot shifted with shocking suddenness that made her call out just before she plunged into the silt-filled flood. Her feet were swept downstream, fluttering out from underneath her in the current. Her right hand burned across the palm as the rope slipped through her clenched fist and her hand tore loose of the guide rope. Both legs kicked as she floundered for footing with her face buried in the creek, sunglasses stripped off and gone, headed west. The icy water stung her eyes and her right shin bashed into a taller piece of granite, sending a blinding pain blasting along the bony edge of her lower leg as she writhed against the pressure.

The rope on her left wrist cut as she desperately held on to her last anchor. Each change in the torrent battered her and her body bounced and twisted like an angry trout on the end of fly-fisher's line.

Bullshit, Becca wanted to scream to the mountains, *this is bullshit,* but she was still face down, mouth clamped shut.

She flung her legs up, thrashing, and regained the top of the granite with a toe this time instead of a shin. She pulled on the strap while she pushed off on her big toe, hunching in the middle to get the other leg down onto something solid.

Contact!

Braced against the flow, Becca pushed her shoulders back just as she felt a powerful grip on her wrist. She convulsed, levering herself into a squatting position, already shouting profanities at the mountain as her face cleared the water.

She panted and stared at her dad, who grasped her arm tight enough to hurt. She was shaking again and an irrepressible determination hardened, combined with a wild fury that she instinctively stoked, broke free.

"I'm doing this!"

She dared him to deny her.

His voice was unsteady but he met her eyes and acquiesced. "No more scaring the dad, Becca-bear." He let go of her wrist and slid his hand back along the rope. He took a solitary step backward.

She rolled her shoulders and twisted her neck before she resumed her crossing. Becca attacked each step. The river still pulled and fought her but Becca fought back.

She reached the other bank and Eagle stood to one side as she pulled herself out of the water, soggy shoes squelching. Her clothes stuck to her skin and her hair was matted but Becca carried her shoulders up and fire burned brightly in her eyes.

"You keep growing up, little bear." Coach Eagle's words

were soft, too low for the others up on dry ground to hear. "Go," he said, indicating the top with his head. "The hard part is over."

Tyler reached down to give her a hand up and she took it.

"You okay?" Dana's voice was shaky. She was pale under her natural complexion.

Becca nodded, not trusting her voice yet. The movement was angry and decisive; her whole body was poised for action, her eyes burning. She stood there, dripping and bedraggled, with a fierceness that made Dana step back.

Becca could feel the change in herself and understood. The veneers she had built up, her camouflage when she wasn't racing, had been washed away by the treachery of the mountain. Gone were the little pretenses and protections of being just another teenage girl that she used to fit in at school to avoid being that odd girl, the one girl—*there was always one girl!*—who was the outcast.

What was left was Becca, sopping wet and tiny but glowing with anger. "*Trust your instincts,*" her father had said. Now she understood that, too. As tightly revealing as the wet shorts and shirt clung, it was the emotional nakedness she felt with the facades washed away, and she accepted it.

She wasn't running away from herself anymore. Ever.

Chapter 14

Rob cut the guideline as he cleared the water and used it to drag himself up the embankment, joining Eagle and the kids. Jim had already undone the end tied to the tree for him. As Rob collected the rope into a bundle his hands were still shaking from watching Becca go under.

The kids stood mutely, observing. Eagle took charge.

"Take a few minutes. If you have any water left that's clean, drink up and get the bottles empty."

He peered at Becca's leg. "You're going to have a heck of a bruise tomorrow. How does it feel?"

Becca, still coming down from the adrenaline rush, looked down at her right shin. She had forgotten it. The area around the impact was already turning purple and blue and the gash trickled blood.

"It hurts." She shrugged.

Eagle considered her answer. "Anybody else got issues?"

A chorus of no's came from the kids as Dana reached out her hand.

"Where's that first-aid kit?"

"I'm okay."

"Sure, but I'm going to wrap it up anyway."

Dana's gaze was steady and it occurred to Becca that in the space of a couple of days, the Hispanic girl from the city had become the kind of friend you kept for life. She unzipped the soggy pack and pulled out the kit.

Eagle turned to Rob and the two of them separated from the group, keeping their voices down but still audible. As Dana tended to her wound, Becca eavesdropped on the men.

"Joseph has the others?" asked her dad.

"I love that kid," said Eagle. "If Gracie is anything like him, she's going to be special."

Becca frowned at the mention of Joseph's cousin, but she couldn't touch the anger she felt at her dad when she heard that he was bringing over another runner to train. A year and she'd move on to college and he could train who he liked.

Eagle was still talking.

"Said he had a bad feeling when the clouds started rolling in, so he grabbed one of the vans and some extra gear to head for the landing. Got there in time to see the lightning, I guess. Anyway, we busted ass getting back to the bridge and he was waiting. I got one squawk on the radio from you about the fire and then a burning tree came over the cliff."

Eagle laughed. "Pretty impressive watching it fall. I figured you were in trouble 'cuz the trail cuts right across the ledge there. Hollered for you to go find the trail around the lake and headed downriver after I got the kids across okay."

His expression became serious.

"Damn glad you got the message about the trail. You can't see it for the trees but the fire's just scorching everything in its path. Smoke must be five thousand feet high already."

Rob was shaking his head.

"Nothing came over the radio." He ran a hand over his scalp. "Becca said she remembered it from the lodge map." He looked pleased. "She's done a hell of a job out here. They all have."

A pleasing warmth washed over her from the compliment and made her smile.

"When we get back, we'll let them roast marshmallows." Eagle checked his watch. "We have plenty of time to sundown. It's a bit more than two and a half miles back. How are they?"

"They all can run. Need to keep the pace down. Dana's getting tired and that whack on Becca's leg is only going to get worse."

Becca saw him glance her way as he said this and she knew that he was letting her overhear the conversation. Dana seemed to be tuning it out as she knelt in front of Becca, applying the finishing touches to the bandage. The boys were quietly talking by the trailhead. Becca watched a huge log sail by, bucking on the choppy surface.

Dana stood up and stepped back to admire her handiwork. She bent forward and pressed a corner of the adhesive tape down where it hadn't stuck properly and then stood again.

"There you go, all better," she said.

The white of the bandage was stark on Becca's dirty, tanned leg. She reached down and rubbed it where it pressed against her calf.

"Itches a little," Becca explained. "Feels better in front though. Thanks."

Rob and Jim had followed the little exchange.

"Time to get moving again," said Jim. The two adults swapped looks and moved to reenter the clearing.

Dana took another step back to give the men room as they crossed the open space to the kids. As she did, Becca's focus was drawn to the girl's position, then to the edge of the embankment just feet away.

"Hey, Dana, you might want to—"

She never completed the statement. A line opened in the dirt. In ultra-slow motion, she watched as Dana's eyes flew open. Becca could see individual grains of sand falling into the growing crevasse. Dana started to shout, tried to lean forward.

Three feet of dirt, undercut by this most recent flash flood, eroded. In geological epochs and with enough erosion, small events led to Grand Canyons, but today it was just one river, a small amount of frail earth, one girl with terrible, frightened eyes, and nothing grand.

The line widened, dark and growing deeper, and the island that Dana was on sunk as she flailed her arms. Larger chunks of earth broke away and gravity inexorably worked to pull it all, along with Dana, to the water.

There was no rumble of an earthquake or thunderclap, just the quiet of the sand slipping away, of fast-moving water, of Dana's desperate intake of breath that she never had a chance to release into a scream—and a quiet splash below.

Chapter 15

Becca lunged for the vacant space Dana had occupied an instant earlier but Rob Hawthorne beat her. He jackknifed himself over the edge, throwing his feet into open space, chasing Dana to the river.

Eagle, close behind, stopped Becca with an arm as she started to follow.

"No!" His eyes burned into hers. He turned to the boys, who were just recognizing the sudden disaster.

"Over here, now!"

He kept a powerful arm around Becca, pinning her against him as they watched Rob slither to the bottom of the embankment, leaving skin on the protruding rocks, landing a few feet from Dana in shallow, fast-moving water flooding over a sandbar.

The stunned girl sat half submerged. Becca watched her expression morph as recognition grew of the danger she had fallen into. A second later, the force of the water sent Dana skittering across the unstable surface, headed downstream a foot at a time. She tried to regain her feet but in her scrambling efforts she only thrashed at the water without getting enough purchase to get upright. She worked more frantically as the sand in the shallow channel she sat in dissolved and was carried away to be deposited on another beach later.

"Dana!"

Rob's voice cut sharply, and her frantic efforts paused as she made eye contact.

Becca heard Jazz and Tyler charge up but couldn't take her eyes off Dana and her father.

"Stay put," he said as he took a tentative step, testing his footing. Becca could see the water roiling around his legs as he moved. He kept his knees flexed and the bunched muscles in his quads quivered. Dana gulped and nodded and quit fighting, which settled her onto the sand. The water was deeper, up to her armpits.

"Get below them," ordered Eagle to the boys. "That way." He pointed.

Both of them froze.

"Move!"

Jazz tore off, Tyler right behind him, headed for the point of land, the tip of the triangle that represented the farthest they could go without recrossing the stream. They skidded to a halt and looked over the edge to watch.

Rob took another step, and then another, and was within an arm's reach of Dana.

"Dana, I'm going to reach out my hand. Grab it and hang on."

He squatted down and extended a wiry arm. Trembling, Dana reached for it—and the river shifted her body another six inches away from him and the shore. The water just covered her chest, leaving her shoulders and head exposed as sand continued to sift out from under her.

Her eyes were luminously dark and wide. They moved quickly, searching for a safe haven, until they came back to Rob's hand, a silent plea for help.

Becca could hear the girl's teeth chattering.

"—*help* . . ."

Becca's breath caught in her throat. A mental picture of Dana's brothers, already motherless, left her knees weak.

"You stay put," Eagle whispered in her ear, and she nodded. He released her and started to move to the broken earth, settling to a knee.

Rob saw him move. He turned his head to speak.

"Wait up there, Jim. I'll get Dana over to the edge and you pull her up." This last part he said to Dana, tone confident.

He moved closer to Dana and his knees disappeared below the surface. He was closer to Dana this time when he extended his hand.

"Just grab my hand. Don't move anything else yet, okay?"

Dana put out her left arm, jerky and tremulous, and leaned to reach Rob.

His strong hand closed around her wrist and her knuckles showed white as she closed her hand, too.

"Now I need you to stand up, but slowly. Lean back and use me as anchor." He paused and forced a smile. "Got it?"

Dana's voice was quaking. "Uh-huh."

She slowly lifted up as he directed, first to her knees and then up to her feet. As she got her back foot settled into the sand, the last grains washed away and her foot slipped into the deeper channel where the flow was relentless. As she pitched backward, her hand flew open and her slender olive-toned wrist twisted away from his grip. A small shriek escaped from Dana as the river moved her towards the faster main channel.

Rob never hesitated. He pitched himself forward, grabbing for Dana's arm. He caught it but the weight of the girl dragged him into deeper, faster water. Already off balance and falling, he launched himself after Dana and wrapped himself around her as the river captured them and they accelerated away from shore.

Becca watched, horrified, as Eagle cursed and sped toward Jazz and Tyler. Jazz was already moving as close to the water as he could get, but Becca tracked the outward-bound arc of Dana and her father. They were going to miss land.

Rob twisted, kicking hard with all the power in his legs, getting Dana's head above water and driving for shore. Dana was thrashing in his arms as the two of them picked up speed. Rob maneuvered again, turning his body, and Becca could see the log, the grayed remains of a tree, between them and the rapids fifty yards downriver. Rob kicked hard to make sure they didn't miss the last safety net.

Rob arched with the impact of the wood into his unprotected back and Becca heard the pain in his grunt. He flung an arm up over the trunk even as the current tried to drag him under. He stayed arched, keeping Dana elevated as she kicked furiously, trying to help.

Jazz hit the base of the sandy cliff and scrambled onto the log. It lurched with his weight but Tyler was right next to him and tried to secure the base.

"Go!" he shouted to his friend.

Jazz slithered out, dodging the stubs of broken limbs as he inched closer to Dana. The log sagged under his weight and Rob readjusted. Becca could see him talking in Dana's ear, but none of the words reached her as she ran to help. Eagle was already down at the log, leaning into it with Tyler.

Dana turned in Rob's arms, an inch at a time, until she was facing him. He rolled his shoulders to get her closer to the tenuous connection to solid ground. She shinnied up his arm to the log and wrapped both of hers around it. Her legs curled under the log as the pressure swept under them.

Jazz reached her.

"Get her out," said Rob, his voice tense. He kept his free hand on Dana's back.

Jazz looked puzzled for a second, then quickly unhooked his run pack. He forced it under her armpits and ratcheted it tight, with only enough slack to insert his hand.

"Easy," he said, and Dana started pulling herself over to land as Jazz fought to keep her head up.

Rob tried to follow but the log moved and he stopped and waited his turn. He kept both arms on the log and let his legs float. Becca could see him puffing from exertion.

Dana got a foot in the mud and attempted to move faster. Jazz kept up the pressure as he worked his way backward. Eagle stepped into the water and extended his arm, reaching below the surface, hooked her by her pack. He dragged her stumbling onto land.

"We got her," he shouted to Rob. "Get your ass in here."

Jazz started to head back out and the log shifted again.

"Wait," said Rob. The boy froze and the log resumed its bobbing, steady rhythms. Rob started moving again and Jazz gently eased himself off the log.

Quiet sobs from Dana wafted up to Becca. The middle of her chest ached and she wanted to comfort the other girl but a quick glance confirmed there wasn't room below.

She glanced at her dad and movement on the river caught the corner of her eye.

A chunk of a tree, eight or ten feet of log, rode the roller coaster of currents, aimed right at Rob.

"DAD, LOOK OUT!"

He shot a startled look up to her and followed her pointing hand out just in time to see the wood. He flung up his left arm, barely in time. The driftwood, driven by the inexorable force of nature, hit him squarely, crushing into the outstretched arm and collapsing it into his body.

Becca heard the crunch of bone breaking in his forearm and his scream as he was torn free. Immediately, he was dragged underneath the supporting log, which took its turn at absorbing impact and, with a grind, broke free. The butt end just missed Eagle and Dana in its ponderous swing, and then it drifted free on the next leg of an ageless journey to the sea.

Rob resurfaced, swept up into the middle of the river, fighting vainly to find something solid, anything solid, to hold on to. As he spun through the water, she saw the arm come clear, bent unnaturally between the elbow and the wrist. He tumbled again in the turbulence and entered the rapids.

Rob hit a rock in the rapids and screamed again, in fury and fear. His momentum surged him past more rocks and, for a brief moment, his eyes locked on to Becca's, and even at that distance, she could see his eyes, a flash of recognition, of love, of regret, and she heard his scream again, but it wasn't his—it was hers, as the connection was broken and he washed out of sight beyond the bend in the river.

Chapter 16

Dana cried softly most of the way back to camp, leaning into Jazz's chest to muffle the sound. He kept an uncomfortable arm around her, uncertainty in every motion, and pity in each glance toward Becca, who sat in the front seat of the van. In the driver's seat, Jim Eagle drove in grim silence and self-recrimination.

Becca had not spoken since Eagle had physically picked her up and started the rest of them marching to the rope bridge. After a torrent of tears, Becca had dried up, huddling inside herself. She had kicked and squirmed her way free of Eagle's grasp, and stomped forward, ignoring everything around her. Dana tried to reach out and comfort her, but Becca shrugged off the hand with a violent twist of her shoulders. She forced past the rest, setting a hard march to the bridge crossing.

The vans sat where the coaches had parked them, the white paint despoiled with gray ash and streaks from the downpour. Becca had crossed on the rope lines mechanically while Eagle watched nervously, hands tight on the safety line. The water rushed nearly at their feet, the level of the river splashing up onto the sandy banks where the bridge abutments sat.

The log perched on the boulder was gone. Becca glared furiously at the now bare rock as she crossed, wondering whether it was the same log that had hit her father.

As the coach slowed to turn off the gravel Forest Service road and onto pavement, Becca could see the tops of the mountains, smoke billowing up and over the passes, orange licks of flame visible on the flanks.

As they fled, the mountains watched impassively and, to Becca, accusingly.

The camp was a riot of activity.

Runners were hustling to gather up all their personal gear from the huts. Staff directed their efforts, the counselors barking instructions, using quick glances at their clipboards to make sure that each runner under their care was accounted for. The van doors were open and the cargo areas were filling quickly. Sandi was at the center of the whirlwind. She shouted instructions and organized the counselors.

Eagle drove the van into the middle of the courtyard and swung it around so it was facing out toward the entrance before he killed the engine. He sat there with his strong hands, dirt embedded into the creases, laid on the wheel. He took a shuddering breath and let it out.

In the backseat, Dana stirred as Tyler jerked on the door handle. He forced it open and climbed down to the ground. Becca unclipped her seat belt and it retracted. She pulled the latch on her door and slid to the ground. She stood in the brilliant sunshine, blinking at the glare from the vehicles.

Sandi saw them drive in and hurried to meet them. Lines of worry creased her face.

"I've got everybody loading up," she said without preamble, speaking past Becca to her husband. "Joseph said the fire was bad, and the Tribe called and said the Forest Service was evacuating everybody."

Jim sat staring ahead as though he hadn't heard. His knuckles were white on the wheel. Sandi glanced around the vehicle, took in the shock on Becca's face and the tears on Dana's. Jazz couldn't meet her eyes. The worry on Sandi's face changed to trepidation.

"What happened, Jim?" she asked. She leaned past Becca and ducked her head into the van. "Where's Rob?"

An anguished sob came from Dana and Jazz held her close.

Becca was still staring into a far, far distance, at the mountains, feeling them surround her.

"He's running a little behind," she said from that remote place and walked away, toward her cabin.

They didn't let her go far. Sandi steered her to the first-aid room and recruited Joseph to watch her until the staff nurse could check on her. The room, like the rest of the camp, was spare. White boxes with red crosses painted on them held the minimal supplies the camp expected to use. If someone in the camp suffered a major injury, they were loaded into a vehicle and sent to the nearest hospital, forty-three miles away. A doctor was closer, his office at the nearest town only a half-hour drive, but cell phone service was horribly unreliable.

"We left him."

Her voice, so low that Joseph almost missed what she said, was calm. She didn't turn to see if he had heard. She stood by the window while he sat, perched on the edge of the folding chair, and waited with his hands folded. If she had looked at him, she would have seen his lips moving.

"He's hurt and we left him," she repeated, and a small crack showed in her control.

Joseph unfolded himself and took two strides across the room to stand at her side, but hesitated when he reached her. Tentatively, he put an arm around her shoulders. She leaned into him, but her attention stayed focused on the view from the window.

"They will find him," he said. "Coach Eagle has already called the Forest Service to report the accident. And he called your mother."

He turned his head as the door opened. Sandi brought Dana into the room and paused when she saw Joseph drop his arm from Becca. She arched an eyebrow but otherwise ignored it.

"The nurse will be here shortly. I want all the kids checked out before we head to Missoula."

Dana wavered and Sandi walked her over to one of the two chairs. Dana shook her head and shrugged Sandi's hand off her arm and went to stand next to Becca. She reached out and grasped Becca's limp hand and squeezed it.

"I'm so sorry," she said. Dana didn't look at Becca, left her with the privacy of her own mind. She just stood there, holding her hand.

A shudder went through Becca's shoulders and her breath came in jerky bursts, but she squeezed Dana's hand and bitter tears finally began to leak.

Forest Service trucks barged into the camp as Becca and Dana walked back to their cabin, accompanied by the nurse.

The first pickup disgorged the honchos carrying computers and shouting into cell phones. The doors to the second and third vehicles whipped open before the gravel stopped popping under the tires, and men rushed to the beds. They pulled out boxes and cases and two antennas and busily began erecting towers.

Jim Eagle came out of the lodge to meet them but Becca watched as they brushed past him, and saw the anger on the coach's face. She turned abruptly and strode toward the lodge.

"Becca," said the nurse, a professionally pleasant woman named Alice. "Why don't you come with me? Those men have work to do." She held Dana by the arm to prevent another escape.

Becca kept walking.

She slithered through the door between men carrying gear boxes. Others inside were already setting up the communications equipment for the Incident Management Team with practiced movements. Amidst the activity, the incident commander, a silver-haired man, stood with a phone pushed against his ear. Eagle waited a few feet from him, fuming.

"Plan on a call-up of the reserve teams," the man said. "We have four reports of lightning strikes with major ignitions—"

He listened.

A burst of static blasted from the dining tables and the technician swiftly reduced the noise.

"We have comms," said a young man in his early twenties as he slipped headphones on.

The IC cocked his head and shot a fast, appraising look at Eagle, still dressed in the dingy running gear.

"I think I have him in front of me," he said into the phone. To Eagle, he asked, "You're with the Tribe?"

"Yes."

As the two men confirmed status, Becca inched closer to the coach until she was standing next to him. Eagle noted her presence with a nod.

"Yeah, got him." While the man listened, he motioned the coach closer with a waggle of two fingers. He lifted the speaker away from his mouth. "How fast can you get these kids out of here?"

The coach frowned. "Thirty minutes, give or take. The staff is getting them moving and they're mostly packed."

This was repeated into the phone. "Tell the first responders to watch for traffic—we've got a butt-load of vans headed back their way."

The man nodded once more and terminated the call. As he did, he transferred the phone over to his left hand and reached forward with his right.

"Mark Greenwood. I'm the incident commander for the fire team. Good to meet you."

He sounded annoyed to Becca.

Eagle shook hands with the man. "Jim Eagle. The Elders asked me to observe."

Greenwood shrugged. "Right, a little odd, normally they just let us do our thing, but that's okay." He looked curiously at Becca before addressing the coach again. "I understand you were out there when everything lit off. Anything you can add that we don't already know?"

Greenwood was a large man and probably good at his job, but Becca didn't like the way he interrogated Eagle. The exchange of information ran in one direction and the commander leaned over them each time he asked a question.

Eagle gave a shake of his head. "Two strikes up on flanks of Como Peaks," he said. He reached out to point out the spot on the map that a crewman had spread on the wooden tabletop. "Right about here." He moved his finger down along the map.

"This is where we lost Rob Hawthorne. How soon until you can get a crew out there for SAR?" he asked, using the jargon for "search and rescue."

"Right," said Greenwood, tracking the finger on the paper, "we know about those, got a spotter plane up. Got a couple more, west of there. Wind's pushing everything this way."

Greenwood looked up at Eagle and he set his face in a neutral expression when he met the shorter man's gaze.

"We can't initiate any rescue attempts until we know what is happening with the fires out there. Once we know what we're dealing with, we can get more proactive, but, until then, I'm not losing crews because we go off half-cocked with lousy intel."

He held the moment a beat and his voice softened. "I understand that there is a man out there that might need our help and I hate to say we can't do anything, but until we have a grasp of the dynamics of these fires, I can't take the chance." He added as an afterthought, "Assuming he's still alive."

All the air sucked out of Becca as the IC talked, and the numbness in her brain expanded to her limbs.

"He's my father." In the same distant voice she'd used when speaking to Sandi, she answered Greenwood. She lifted her face up to him and her cheeks flushed, hot against the deadness of her skin. "And he's alive."

Greenwood scowled and his skin blotched as he shifted his eyes to the coach. "You brought her in *here*?"

"She followed you in, not me—"

"I don't care how she got in here, she's out right now and you can get out with her. I'll be damned if I'll let you guilt me into losing good men on a lost cause!"

Becca's eyes flew open and mouth gaped open at Greenwood's bluntness. She snapped it shut and clamped her jaws together so hard that the muscles ached with the strain as she fought for breath.

Eagle recovered faster than she did. He shushed her with a look and responded to Greenwood, his voice filled with ice.

"First, the Tribe owns this facility and I am their representative, so you will not be throwing me out. Second, your assumption that Rob Hawthorne is dead does not fit with your mission and you know it, so you will mount a search and rescue"—he raised a palm flat in front of the commander to keep him from objecting—"when it is safe for you to do so. Third, you will treat this young lady with respect as you will treat all persons here with respect. Now, what do you need of me to move forward with your mission?"

Greenwood seethed but said as gracefully as he could, "Get out of my way and let me do my job—before we lose more people, fire crew or hikers." His eyes got narrow and mean. "Get her out of here. And, if you want to watch, you can do it from over there." He nodded to the corner of the dining hall, banishing the coach like a particularly recalcitrant child.

"If I need anything, I'll let you know. Just stay out of my way."

Chapter 17

Dana sat in a rickety chair with an old and familiar ache heavy in her chest. She had washed her face, removing the trails of tears on her cheeks, but her eyes got wet as she visualized Coach Hawthorne carried away in the maelstrom and heard his cries again. Deep memories she thought were gone thrust up, a swirl of pictures accompanied by the poignant simplicity of childhood, reminding her of when her mom passed. At first, it was disbelief and shock, the image of the man telling her, and the crushing effect it had on her dad. Then, anger, bitterness at the gross unfairness. More phases—depression and acceptance—came and passed but a wound deep inside her never fully healed. . . .

The door to the cabin was open and Dana watched as Becca stormed across the courtyard. In Becca's stride, she read that dangerous anger. Dana blinked quickly. It seemed to help, maybe a little bit.

Along with the memories came the resolve, that strength that let her become the woman of the family, to help raise the boys.

She watched Becca approaching and her heart broke a little bit for her new friend. Never would she have wished this on anyone, and Becca, for all the anger and pride, looked so small and lonely as she crossed into the cabin.

Becca looked at Dana with an impenetrable air of defiance as she entered and crossed to her bunk. She dropped the run pack in her left hand while reaching up with the right to grab her bag. She dragged it down onto the lower bunk and began rummaging through it, pulling out clean clothes. She set them out on the rumpled bedding but stood there, just looking at them.

"Do you want some help packing?" asked Dana.

Becca leaned forward and rested her head against the side rail of the bunk bed. She didn't respond.

"I'm sorry," said Dana. "I'm so, so sorry."

Becca was turning her head side to side, rolling over the spot on her forehead that touched the wood of the bed frame.

"They're not going to look for him." Becca enunciated each word with contempt.

"Why not?"

"Because, as the man said, he's not going to waste more lives to try and find him." Becca banged her head against the frame—*tap, tap, tap*—not hard, and her breaths came out shuddering from the suppressed rage. She looked up suddenly. "They think he's already dead."

Dana gulped and bit down on the inside of her lower lip while her chest trembled. The chair creaked and grumbled as she got up and crossed the gap to Becca. She put a hand on Becca's shoulder.

Becca dipped the shoulder slightly and turned away from the pressure.

"No," she said, and moved away to stand by the window, looking out past the activity in the yard as the last of the camp vans filled with panicky teenagers anxious to leave. She heard Dana sniffle and knew that Dana was feeling guilty, because she felt it too and she hadn't fallen into the damn river. Or, at least, when she had, she had pulled her own ass out. As Becca thought this, a little voice reminded her that she fell in the creek, not the river, and that she had a handhold and Dana didn't, and that her dad, just like with Dana, had followed her into the water.

"It's not your fault, you know," she said, eyeballs still locked on the purposeful motion in front of her.

"I keep telling myself that," said Dana, "but if I hadn't fallen . . ." The girl lapsed into silence and an uncomfortable void existed between them.

Becca knew that she had to avoid climbing into one of those vans. Once the staff loaded her on, she would be forced to go to Missoula and, once there, made to wait for her mother to make the long journey from North Carolina to Montana. The entire time, she would be waiting, dreading news of her dad and hating the knowledge that they wouldn't even search for him until it was too late.

Becca felt it deep in her gut, he was alive. There had been too much fury in his eyes to lie down and die in the river. A picture of his arm, twisted at the forearm, formed and she shivered. He was alive but the night would be cold and he would be wet. She knew that he would have extra food in the run pack. He always carried extra. *But not enough for days of survival, not enough to generate the body heat to fight the chill Montana air after dark.*

And, after the sun fell, the predators would be roaming. She had seen the remains of a white-tailed deer after the wolves, and she shivered again. Maybe the fire had driven them off, she thought, but her mind drifted back and catalogued the others: mountain lions, solitary and happy to attack wounded prey; bears, advantageous; even rattlesnakes, who wouldn't want to strike but would to protect themselves from an oblivious stumbling man.

She couldn't get into a van.

Becca turned from the window and sidestepped past Dana to get to the bunk. She sat and opened her run pack and began to unload it, spreading the contents across the mattress. Dana moved to her left to make room and turned to face her.

Becca saw she still had the bandage on her arm. Scratches adorned her legs, fine lines beaded with tiny droplets of dried blood on the tanned skin, and everything with a layer of dust and ash; her thick black hair, so lustrous that morning, was dingy and stringy. Her eyes, though, were alive and caring, and Becca couldn't look at them too long, so she looked away, down to the small items that belonged in the run pack. She sorted them and made a mental note to pull out more rope.

"You'll need to hurry up," said Dana, as she walked to her bags situated near the bunk. She sat next to Becca. "They want us out of here like yesterday."

Her voice wasn't nagging, just firm. *A mom voice,* thought Becca. Dana was used to bossing boys around, her brothers, and she was taking control of her newest wayward waif.

Becca kept her head turned toward her gear bag and reached in, selecting a pair of long run pants and a pink top made from technical fabric. A spare length of line, tightly wound, joined the other implements on the bed.

"Do you think the bear made it?"

Dana rocked backward slightly as she fielded the question and some of Becca's gear shifted and slid.

"I don't know," said Dana. "I hope so."

Becca reached out and gathered up her stuff as her friend answered. She loaded the run pack with the knife and a clean bandana and a new piece of rope. The first-aid kit went in as well and Becca zippered it shut.

"I keep thinking about his eyes," said Becca, and she paused but didn't cry. *His eyes!*

Dana touched her at the elbow with her fingertips, misunderstanding.

"The bear was beautiful, Becca, but we got to go."

"I hope he made it. He was headed in the right direction, cutting across the wind."

Dana reached around Becca and scooped up the loose clothing. Becca grabbed her run pack and pulled it to her side, the opposite side from Dana. She stood and stripped off her shirt, ignoring the open door, and pulled the clean pink one over her head. The long pants she carried in a hand over the run pack.

"I want to say good-bye to Uncle Jim."

"I'll carry your bag out to the van and meet you out there?" Dana's voice rose at the end, adding a question mark to the statement.

Becca nodded and left the cabin. As she turned toward the lodge, she saw Jazz coming. The boy was freshly scrubbed and his hair damp. His legs looked like someone had flogged him with a slender whip, lashes at all angles from the bottom of his shorts to the tops of his socks. In the fading light of the day, tingeing the haze that engulfed everything in tints of red and orange, they looked raw and painful. He diverted briefly as though he were going to intercept her but, reading her frown, seemed to change his mind.

She dropped the pants and the run pack on a bench before she reached the door. As she reached for the knob, she could hear the hubbub of voices and static of the radios.

The handle was warm in her hands, heated by the unseen sun, and turned smoothly. She swung the door open, eyes trying to adapt to the dimness in the room. Light poured around her and a shadow longer than she would ever be tall stretched out on the floor, but she did not cross the threshold, honoring Greenwood's injunction.

"Uncle Jim?" she called out, her feminine voice starkly contrasted with those of the fire crew operators.

Eagle was where she had last seen him, standing in the corner. He stood relaxed with his arms crossed, leaning into the wall. He caught sight of her, framed against the light of the doorway, and, with a shove against the wood, stood straight and walked her way. She stepped back as he reached her and he closed the door behind him. He stood in front of her, silent and waiting.

Becca wasn't sure how to start. She looked down to see that she was fumbling with the bottom of her shirt, rolling the edge between her fingers.

"Uncle Jim," she began, without looking up, "do they have any word on my dad?"

He sighed. "Not so far." Even tones and a noncommittal attitude, but with an undercurrent of compassion.

She struggled to draw in a breath. *Are they even looking?* she wanted to shout—but she kept her head down. She hunched her shoulders down lower and her fingers stayed busily at work.

"Are you going to stay here until they find him?" She still hadn't looked up to see what he was thinking. "Someone should be here when they bring him in, one of us."

A long silence and then the coach answered.

"I'd planned on it."

Becca scuffed a shoe across the decking, watching it catch on the gaps between the planks.

"Is my mom going to pick me up in Missoula?"

"We called her and she's grabbing the first plane this way, but Sandi will know more. You should ask her."

"Is Aunt Sandi staying there with me? I don't want to stay with strangers . . ." She let her voice taper off to a whisper. ". . . not now."

He grunted, and started to answer, but she interrupted.

"Can I stay here with you?" This time she did peek up, to gauge his reaction. There was none and she looked down again. Her voice picked up a hint of desperation. She took a deep breath and the words began to spurt out.

"I want to stay close to him. I know what Mr. Greenwood said, and I'll be good and stay out of the way but I want to be here when they bring him in. He's hurt really bad and needs to have family here and Mom's too far away so that leaves it up to us and I'm his daughter." She grabbed another lungful of air. She would have tried for tears but knew that if she started, she'd never stop, so she channeled it into her words.

"Please let me stay, just until my mom gets here and then we can wait together except they'll find him before that so I just have to be here because there's no one else, family I mean," Becca hurried to reassure him, "not that you're not like family but I'm his daughter." She stopped to grab more air.

Eagle held up a single hand. "Stop."

He was shaking his head.

"Just . . . stop."

Becca closed her mouth and stared at him in dejection. A boulder seemed stuck in her chest and was slowly crushing everything below it and she suppressed a tremor in her hands, still fiddling with the hem.

He was looking at her thoughtfully.

She shifted her gaze. It was thirty yards to the tree line. She could make it if nobody was watching, then wait for dark.

"You can stay, on two conditions."

Her head snapped back. "Anything!"

"First, you keep your promise about Greenwood. There's a half a dozen hiking parties that they've identified already that are in the path of that fire and we're not going to do anything that distracts them from saving those people. You stick your nose in where it doesn't belong and you'll be headed out of here before you can blink."

"—yes, sir."

"Second rule, you do everything I say when I say it—and that includes leaving if I say it's time for us to bug out, even if we don't have Rob back yet."

She closed her eyes and dropped her head. She didn't want to lie to his face.

"Will you tell Aunt Sandi for me?"

He snorted. "Oh sure, so she can yell at me instead of you?"

Becca waited.

"Fine," he said, but with mock resignation. "Wait here."

He strode over to the vans, crossing the dusty lot, his shadow squatter and more powerful than hers. He reached the lead van, piloted by his wife, and started talking to her through the open window. Sandi shook her head and anger flashed across her face. Eagle answered her, using his hands in a wide gesture that made it seem as though he was trying to placate her.

Sandi had her hand out the window, pointed right at Eagle, and her eyes were narrowed. He spread his hands wider in a *Who me?* gesture. His wife said something else and this time, Eagle nodded his head.

He walked over to another van and leaned in. A moment later, the passenger door on the opposite side opened and Joseph walked around the rear of the van. Eagle met him there as the Kenyan man lifted the handle on the rear door and opened it wide. He dug through the piled bags until he located his and dragged it out.

The two of them walked back toward Becca. Behind them, the last of the doors slammed shut and the engines started, one after the other.

"Joseph has volunteered to stay behind," explained Eagle. Becca doubted the volunteer part but the crushing stone got a lot smaller and she was glad he was with her. Joseph was family, too.

Eagle turned to Joseph.

"Your only job is to keep her"—he pointed to Becca with his chin while locking eyes with the young man—"out of trouble."

"Yes, sir," said Joseph.

Eagle looked at them both one more time as though he wanted to say something else, but shook his head instead, and entered the lodge to see how the search fared.

Dana was sandwiched between the window and Jazz when Eagle came over to his van. The buzz of conversation hushed when he leaned in through the window.

"Joseph," he said, "got a job for you."

"What do you need for me to do?" Joseph said, already unsnapping his seat belt.

"Babysitting duty. Becca's staying."

Now the sound in the van went from quiet to silent. Joseph half-turned in his seat, hesitated only a slow heartbeat, and inclined his head. The noise of the mechanics of the door was loud in the vacuum and the door slamming shut louder still.

Dana twisted to watch when she heard the rear door open. It only took a couple of seconds for Joseph to locate his gear bag, marked with the Bridger emblem. The whole van moved as the door shut solidly with an air-compressing thump. Ahead of them, the lead van started its engine. The counselor driving them did likewise and the sound of the big engine turning over and rumbling to life broke the silence inside the van and the kids began talking again, half excited by the distant danger.

Of the dozen runners in the van, only Dana, Jazz, and Tyler were silent. Tyler was staring out the window from the bench in front of them while Jazz alternated between looking at Dana to losing himself in a stoic stare through the front windshield. Twice he had tried to start a conversation and both times it petered out.

Dana felt drained, as though someone had opened her up to remove all but a flicker of her vitality. She ached all over and knew that Jazz was hurting though the goof wouldn't admit it. The nurse had administered salve to the worst of his cuts and said she would call ahead to have a doctor available when they got to Missoula. Dana knew that she would be on the waiting list, too; so would Tyler.

Worse, she dreaded the other people that would be brought in, the grief counselors who would pick and prod and encourage her to talk it out, *You'll feel better if you do, dear.* Except she hadn't been ready to move on, to say good-bye. Eyes blurry again, she leaned her head against the warm glass, away from the press of people.

The van bucked as the driver put the transmission into drive and lurched when he released the brake and switched to the accelerator. As the slow promenade circled the dusty parking lot, she saw Becca walking back to the cabins. She watched as Becca stopped, not to watch the vans leaving without her, but to stare to the west.

Dana felt a coldness grow as she watched Becca through the long arc of leaving.

Dana almost called out to the driver to stop, to go back. Almost but didn't, because Becca would never forgive her and no grief counselor would ever be able to reach that place where the real Becca lived.

Becca had that look, the one Dana knew would never be on her own face. It was that same expression she'd had when she had erupted from the water cursing the mountain and the forest and the fire. Dana could feel the power flowing from Becca, the indomitable spirit captured in a tiny form, standing alone in the gravel.

Swinging in Becca's hand was her run pack.

Becca stopped in the dust as the vans turned onto the road. She didn't look at them, didn't want to watch her friends leave. Instead, she stared up into the murk to where the mountains waited and watched. *We are still here, we will always be here,* they whispered in her brain. *We endure.*

She stared and she heard them and it didn't matter because she was going out there anyway. He was alive, and she was going to bring him back, and nothing the mountain could do would stop her.

Hawthornes don't quit.

Chapter 18

After the vans left, Becca went to the cabins. Dana had taken her bags as she promised, which left Becca with no bedding or clean clothes except the shirt and pants. It was too hot to wear those yet. She went to her dad's cabin and borrowed his soap and a towel so she could take a shower. Her legs ached and a hot, soaking spray would loosen them up.

She stripped down and let the hot stream from the nozzle do its work on her shoulders and back while she rinsed her sports bra and wrung it out. In the steam, she plotted out each step of her plan. The water smelled tinny from the metals in the groundwater well that supplied the camp.

She needed to grab her dad's truck keys and stash them in with her other trail gear. She was nervous about driving at night on the unfamiliar roads but she had her license and knew how to read a map. She'd find the best spot down the river to start her search, drive to it, and get her dad back to the truck.

Done with the bra, she started to rinse her shorts, a surprising amount of sand depositing on the bottom of the shower as she did so.

The nurse had forced some food on her earlier but now her appetite reasserted itself and she was ravenous. After the shower, she needed to eat. A pang of guilt at the thought of eating while her dad was still lost bit deep but she shook it off. It wasn't food—it was fuel, absolutely necessary if she was to function later. She'd eat after the shower.

Her thoughts veered again, always back to her dad. He would need food. Some she could bring on the trail, high-energy foods, the rest could stay locked in the truck. It would be safe from animals if she locked it in. She should definitely pack some into her run bag.

Becca turned to bring her left shoulder fully into the spray, trying to get it to loosen. All the muscles from her wrist to the shoulder ached from the dunking in the creek. The palm of her other hand had a pretty good rope burn but she would put some more antiseptic ointment on it and cover it with a clean bandage.

She reached up and grabbed the supply pipe for the shower and twisted and the muscles stretched. Good enough, she figured.

Becca hadn't looked in the truck yet to see if there were maps inside. Most likely there were, knowing her dad, but when no one was looking, she would check. If there weren't any in the truck, she would need to get into the lodge and borrow some of theirs.

She had no idea how she could get in the lodge room, much less stay there long enough to steal a map without them knowing, but that would be a worry for later. First, check the truck.

Crap, she thought. *Do I have enough gas? Only need enough to get downriver and back.* If she made it back to the camp, she could get gas or use a different vehicle.

She turned up the hot water as high as she could stand and the steam billowed out over the top of the shower stall.

Medical kit. She had a first-aid kit. Her dad was hurt, his arm broken at a minimum, probably more wrong with him after the river. Plus exposure. *Check his kit in the truck.* She thought about trying to swipe supplies from the med room and immediately abandoned the idea. Most of the important stuff was locked up tight and she had to pass right next to the tables with the radios. No way Greenwood would miss her, and Uncle Jim would be watching every move. *No bueno,* as Dana would say.

Eyes closed, she let the water beat down on her head, running down her body. Her knees got wobbly as she considered the magnitude of her plan, so she leaned into the shower stall wall and went over it again, piece by piece, looking for holes in the jigsaw.

The light bled in along the bank of windows set high on the walls. Two hours until sunset, another hour until full dark. She knew that she was missing things, details that were important, and understood she didn't have any more time to plan. Time was sprinting away while she soaked in the shower.

Becca pushed off the wall and quickly turned off the water. The mineral smell dissipated and was replaced with wood smoke. Using the towel, she winced as she rubbed briskly, the scratchy nap of the fabric leaving her skin feeling refreshed but abrading the dozens of small slashes that had been inflicted by the branches. She gave the sports bra another twist and slipped it over one arm. Her skin rebelled at the touch of the clammy, confining material. It would be dry in an hour if she hung it out. She held on to it a bit longer, contemplating slipping it on anyway. There was hardly anybody here, though. She put it aside instead and slipped the pink run shirt back on, and then put on her long pants. The wet shorts joined the bra. She slipped into her shoes, feeling the grit on the inserts. She bundled her damp clothes in the towel and went to the nearest mirror to run a brush through her hair, leaving it straight. She pulled it back into a quick, sloppy ponytail.

Good enough.

When she got back to the cabin, she placed the running shorts and bra on the back of a chair to dry. The towel was discarded to the floor. She liberated her dad's keys from his bag. Becca quickly tucked the tag of the keychain into the waistband of her pants.

The parking lot was eerily quiet as she went to the lodge. As she walked, the strong gusts pushed the cloth of her shirt snug against her skin, sliding over it, and filled and lifted the bottom as the air plucked at the clothing. The wind was worst in the middle of the lot, where she was most exposed. She looked to see if anybody was watching. The parking lot was empty, the familiar vans replaced by trucks painted Forest Service green. Two of them bore the emblems of the Lolo Hotshots. The fire crews had arrived while she showered. Crossing her arms as though she was hugging herself, Becca hurried up.

She dodged around the end of the building and walked to the rear door that led to the food prep and kitchen areas. The door squeaked as she eased it open. Empty, so she went in. Boxes of food were still stacked up along the rear wall. She opened the large refrigerator and looked inside. She grabbed a gallon of milk and swung the door shut with a thud, putting the jug on the nearest table.

She scrounged through the boxes. The best she could do without cooking was peanut butter and jelly, so she laid out four slices of bread and lathered on a thick coat of peanut butter on two slices, then retrieved the grape jelly from the fridge. She slathered on a layer of jelly on top of the peanut butter, and then closed up the sandwiches with the remaining two slices of bread. She hefted one and took a bite.

The sugar hit her taste buds and her mouth watered as hunger pangs, absent in her worry, reasserted themselves. She devoured the two sandwiches, washing them down with milk. She was leaning a slender hip against the sink peeling a banana when the outside door opened and Joseph stepped inside. He looked relieved.

"It is good that you are eating," he said. His voice was even softer than normal and his features were set in lines of concern, eyebrows creased.

Becca paused before taking a bite of the banana.

"I'm no good to Dad if I pass out from hunger," she said. "It's fuel."

The words came out sounding harsher than she meant, and she saw they stung. He stood across the counter from her for a moment before, with a sigh, he stepped to a cabinet and took out a plastic cup of his own. He filled his with water. He stared at her as he sipped from the cup.

"They will be looking for him soon," he said. "The men are here now who will go fight the fire. They will look." He spoke over the cup, guardedly neutral as he came around the end of the counter to stand closer to her.

"Not soon enough." Becca stood up straight and the top of her pants dragged on the lip of the sink. The batch of keys pulled free of the waistband and they landed on the floor with a clink.

She quickly bent forward to retrieve them. The fabric of her shirt, cut in a V-neck, billowed open as she felt the weight change, her smallish breasts not restrained from gravity. A hand clutched to the opening, hitting mostly skin as the smooth pink of the fabric fell away. It felt as though the entire shirt had gaped open into the air. Her face and ears flushed hot as she hastily tucked a leg under her instead and knelt to pick up the keys.

"I needed—" she said, looking up as she invented an excuse for having the keys. Her skin felt hot and tight.

His eyes shifted and he stared expressionlessly at the keys in her hand.

Wooly-headed thoughts chased each other around her head as she tried to find a lie that would work for the keys while simultaneously explaining the ickiness of a wet bra and all of it hoping to hell this was the worst dream she had ever had, every bit of it.

Though Joseph was not a large man, she felt small next to him and she clenched the keys tight in her fist as she crossed her arms, bunching up the shirt, then uncrossed them, letting the material fall naturally, to cover and disguise. Hand shaking, she took a sip of milk. It helped her suddenly dry mouth and cooled the back of her throat.

Joseph spoke first, oddly formal as he gazed at the boxes of provisions, reading their labels maybe.

"You are not waiting." He still was not looking at her. There was no judgment in his voice, just a simple recitation of the facts.

"I have to." She waited and listened to her heart, each thump loud in her ears. *Please, Joseph,* she thought but did not say, *please don't stop me.*

And an added thought, *And please don't say anything about . . .* and her face exploded with heat again as she felt the thinness of the fabric covering her.

"You will need help." Now he turned and his voice was reproachful. "You should have asked me."

Becca couldn't sleep. She was lying on top of her dad's sleeping bag and his scent lingered. Each time she closed her eyes and drifted off, she slipped into dreams of him, showing up in her classroom in the first grade every Wednesday, because that was pizza day, and eating with her, or the first race she ran when she was five, doing a kids' mile and he ran next to her the whole way, cheering her on. Then she would jerk wide awake as her subconscious went to work replaying the scene of him at the river.

She groaned and sat up, abandoning the attempt at sleep.

She looked out the window. The last glow of twilight was fading on the horizon. When it was gone, it would be time for her to leave. She had swapped the long pants for the now-dry shorts and thrown the bra back on, feeling more secure as she did.

Becca left the lights off as she padded out into the dark in her socks. Beside her, the chair that Joseph had dragged out and set up by the door creaked. She could only see a shadow of him as he stood. The camp sat dark with only the illumination streaming from the windows of the lodge and dying into the night.

"It is almost time."

Becca nodded her head, stopped because Joseph wouldn't be able to see it.

"Yeah."

She didn't ask if he had slept. He had asked her to try to sleep and then paradoxically told her that he would stay awake outside the door and watch.

The wind blew in their faces. The fire was breathing and growing. The superheated smoke expelled into the atmosphere caused air to rush in to replace it. The horizon glowed, the setting sun replaced by smaller, closer conflagrations. They were too far from the fires themselves to see the flame leaping on the wind but Becca could picture it. Her stomach twisted as it had up on the trail as she and her dad had looked down on the early hungry flames.

Joseph had gone into the lodge to get more information while she rested.

The fires were growing with the wind and moving fast but when he looked at the tactical maps in the command post, he said, they showed that the road was clear all the way to the next bridge. He couldn't get copies of the maps, but Becca had found a set of topos in the cabin, neatly trimmed and folded in a plastic baggie. She sorted them into sequence along the river, putting those in order so she could separate them by touch. The others she discarded to the floor.

"I put extra batteries in the packs," said Becca.

She heard slow, measured breaths from him and the rustle of fabric as he stretched.

"Good." A swishing sound, and the shadow rotated through his hips.

Lying down had been a bad idea. Her brain felt fuzzy. She tried to emulate Joseph, moving into the warm-up exercises she used before races. She stopped when the muscles protested.

The antennas the fire crews had set up reflected light dully. Through them, the men inside directed the field crews, seeking some angle of attack, an edge that would begin the process of containing the forest fire. They knew that her dad was out there. It was their job to save him. If she waited, the hotshots, the nickname for the young men who trained zealously for months for the job of standing in the way of nature's fastest destroyer, could find him.

The door opened as someone slipped out and a burst of chatter, businesslike, could be heard. Becca got a brief glimpse of the men working, hunched by the electronics. A truck door squeaked as it was opened, the dome light briefly visible, and slammed shut. The unfamiliar man opened the door again, releasing more chatter, and then the door closed behind him.

She rubbed her face with both hands and inhaled.

"We should go," she said. Her voice was quiet. Hopefully, Joseph couldn't hear the quiver, not just in her voice but in her limbs that threatened to hold her here, waiting. *It's their job.*

He didn't answer but she could feel him looking at her. Becca turned and went into the cabin and retrieved the packs. She grabbed the long pants, just in case she changed her mind. Holding everything in one hand, she used the other to take a long drink of water from the bottle by the bed, draining it, and went back outside.

She handed Joseph the spare pack and let the weight of hers drag her arm down until the straps touched the ground.

"Do you want me to drive?" asked Joseph.

The keys sat heavy in her waistband again. She reached for them and squeezed them.

"Here."

He took the keys from her but didn't move, waiting for her to commit and leaving her a chance to change her mind.

She roused herself. "Let's go."

They moved stealthily along the front of the cabin. Her dad's truck was parked on the side away from the lodge but they would have to drive out in front of the fire crew and Eagle. Becca planned on keeping the lights off until they reached the road so they'd be going slow, but she worried that someone would investigate the noise of the truck rolling on the gravel as they left.

Becca kept a hand touching the wood of the cabin. The pale white of her dad's truck appeared as they pivoted around the corner and out of sight.

She heard a click and a bright light exploded in her eyes and she flinched back.

From behind the light blinding her, she heard a sardonic voice, not loud but filled with steel, slice through the night.

"Well, you are your father's daughter, now, aren't you?"

Chapter 19

"And she roped you in, too."

The light moved and played over Joseph before dropping to their waists. Behind the beam, Becca saw the outline of Jim Eagle. Tears formed in her eyes and her mouth set itself in a thin, bitter line. A hard shake of her head cleared the tears. She sought the coach's eyes, needing the connection.

Her eyes still dazzled, Becca began talking.

"I didn't," she protested. "He saw the keys and guessed—"

"That you would do something dumb and head out into the woods by yourself? Boy, that took a lot of guessing."

Becca missed it and started to talk again.

"I can't just wait here. . . ." She floated to a stop when she heard Joseph laughing, a deep and slow *heh, heh, heh.*

Her breath came in pants, quick and uneven, and her face got tight. She spun toward him.

"It's not funny!" She heard the hopelessness in her own voice, and the skin on her face got tighter. She had stomped her foot as she spoke and that pissed her off even more. Without thinking, she hit Joseph, not a slap but not a punch either, and he rolled with it, but he stopped laughing.

"That will be quite enough of that," said Eagle.

Becca spun back toward the light, now aimed at their feet, shining on the trail-running shoes they both wore.

"Rebecca." Joseph's voice was low and amused.

She stepped forward to confront the coach when Joseph took firm hold of her upper arm.

"*Rah-becca.*" He accentuated her name, his accent more pronounced. "He did not catch us."

Becca leaned away from him and pulled her arm free.

"Think, Rebecca. He is here, at the truck. He could have asked for your keys at any time. And there is no more reason for him to be here than you. He cannot help with the men fighting the fire."

Becca couldn't see his eyes but the intensity of his words came through clearly. He stepped forward to stand close to her.

"He did not *catch* us," he repeated. "He was *waiting* for us."

"And another thirty minutes, I'd been gone without you. Time's a-wasting."

The spots left by being half blinded by Eagle faded as Becca's eyes finally adjusted. In the reflected illumination, she could see the coach and Joseph. The anger at getting caught had burned out, but inside, she was empty. She glanced from Joseph to Eagle and back to the ground. She felt like a dullard and didn't care.

"Are we going to go get my Dad?"

"We will if you'll just get into the truck." Eagle looked at Joseph. "I assume you're going, too?"

"Yes, sir." His smile gleamed. "I was told that I was to keep Rebecca out of trouble, so I must follow her."

"Well, I was told the same thing by my wife and she's going to have both our hides when this is all over."

Joseph pulled open the passenger door and waited for Becca while Eagle went to the driver's side. Becca walked over without a word, reaching high to grab the handhold and climb into the tall rig. She wriggled across the bench seat until she was almost in the middle, sandwiched between the coach and Joseph. Eagle turned the key and the big diesel rumbled to life.

"I've got supplies by the kitchen," he said over the noise.

"We have food in the back," Becca answered automatically, staring out the windshield. "And some maps and my dad's first-aid kit."

"Good girl. Figured you would, but I've got plenty more, just in case."

He looped around the building and left the truck idling while he and Joseph hopped out and lifted three boxes into the back and secured them with a bungee cord. They added a case of bottled water and two five-gallon camp jugs with more water. Eagle tore open the plastic wrap on the case and grabbed half a dozen bottles by the caps and tossed them into the cab of the truck.

"Start drinking."

He went back out and pulled something out of the nearest box. He jumped back into the driver's seat and threw a placard on top of the dash.

"Crap." He dropped back down to the ground and dug into another box.

"Here, hang on to this," he said as he passed Becca a radio.

She turned on the radio with a click and the white noise of static filled the interior of the vehicle. She looked at the settings and saw that it was on channel eight.

"Better save the battery. The charger left with Sandi and the rest of the stuff."

She snapped it off.

"Okay, last chance," Eagle said.

Becca moved away from the stick shift, closer to Joseph, as Eagle slipped the transmission into first gear.

"If you want out, now's the time to say so. Becca?"

"Go."

"Joseph?"

"You will need us both. I will go with Becca."

Eagle leaned forward, foot still planted on the clutch.

"Need you?"

Becca could see Joseph's smile reflected in the windshield, distorted and wider than normal by the curvature of the glass.

"That is why you let Rebecca stay. A single man cannot help an injured man as well as a team."

Eagle looked startled and then gave a low chuckle.

"When you're CEO of that commodities firm, remember that you learned everything from me, okay? And an endowment would be nice."

"Yes, sir," said Joseph, with a straight face.

Becca was still staring out the windshield. As Eagle slipped the clutch and got the large pickup rolling, she asked, "You knew?"

"Of course," Eagle answered.

"You are a very bad liar," offered Joseph.

Eagle drove out of the lot, grinding second gear a bit. The headlights lit up the road as he hit the high beams. To Becca, it seemed they were in a tunnel as the smoky air closed around them.

"Why did you let me stay?"

Eagle glanced at her as he shifted.

"You were eyeing the woods. Short of tying you up and strapping you into the van, I was pretty sure that I couldn't get you to go with the rest of the gang." He squinted as he studied the road. He added thoughtfully, "And I'm playing a hunch."

They drove on in silence. *A hunch?* A brief moment of curiosity penetrated the big empty space inside her but she didn't care enough to ask more. She didn't care. They were on the road to find her dad and that was good enough.

The thrumming of the tires on the road and the vibration were lulling her and soothed her. Becca leaned sideways into Joseph as Eagle negotiated a curve. He stiffened at first before relaxing. His shoulder was warm and she didn't move back. His breath was steady and slow and she listened to it. She didn't understand why exactly he was here but it made her happy that he was.

In the quiet, the dream sequence started again: Dana's face as she fell, her dad hurtling into the river to save her, the log hitting him. She could smell the smoke again, pungent, and painful on her eyes even though she knew she was in the truck and Eagle was driving and her eyes were closed.

The final part of the dream started, her dad bouncing off a rock in the rapids. She could feel herself quivering against Joseph's shoulder and then a hand on her knee as Joseph whispered to her.

"We will find him, Rebecca."

This time, she didn't jerk awake staring at her dad's eyes. They held each other's gaze and then he was gone, around the turn of the river. She imagined him struggling against the current, one arm useless. He would have aimed for shore. This shore because there was no trail on the other side, no hope of help. She saw him angle his body on a slanted line to use the

146

current to push him toward solid ground, saving his fading strength as much as he could.

The climb out of the water would be excruciating. Even if there was a bench of sand above the flood, getting upright with only one arm would send jolts of agony through the body. Every step would jostle the arm, grate the bones over each other. And the forest waited, with its grasping limbs and hidden trip hazards.

She moaned and the hand on her knee squeezed again.

Her imagination failed when she got to the woods, to the first time he fell. The pictures of her dad blended with the furious retreat down the mountain and, unbidden, she could see the damage to Jazz's legs, what the trees and brush had done to a strong, healthy body.

"Don't quit, Daddy."

Eagle shifted in his seat. "He doesn't quit," he said.

She gave a short dismissive snort. Becca hadn't realized that she had spoken aloud. The coach's words were quiet and comforting, and helped to fill some of the emptiness she felt, but she knew he was wrong. He had quit. He quit racing when he was so close. . . .

The struggle at the edge of the woods faded from her mind, and she lost the tenuous connection to her father. She sat up, fully awake again. Joseph removed his hand, folding it with the other in his lap.

She didn't look to Eagle but kept her eyes focused on the hazy world in the lights. Becca knew what she needed to do. Even if he wasn't there, she had to try.

Becca caught Eagle's reaction to the snort in the reflection in the tempered glass of the windshield. He shot a sharp glance at her and, in the distortion of the glass, she read his anger.

"Your dad never quit a damn thing in his life," Eagle said.

Becca retorted before she had a chance to think. "He quit racing!" She paused and the pent-up anger that worry and fear had restrained engulfed her.

"After you beat him, he quit. He keeps telling me '*don't quit, don't quit, don't quit*' and stands there saying '*you only get one shot, so make it count, there aren't any second chances*' and he's right, for him."

She caught her breath and started again.

"But I'm not him. I'm not going to quit, not now, not ever."

The anger flamed out and a wave of despair replaced it. Deep inside, she knew that she was on an emotional roller coaster, and she wanted off, but the operator refused to hit the stop button and the ride wouldn't end.

Out of the corner of her eye, she could see Eagle's knuckles standing starkly white on the steering wheel. A deep, unpleasant silence filled the cab with Becca caught between the anger of Eagle on her left and Joseph's uncomfortable embarrassment on the right. She sat ramrod stiff and refused to look at either. From the periphery of her vision, she saw the slight movement of Eagle's hands as he relaxed them, then extended the fingers wide, pointing over the dash before they closed around the wheel again.

When he spoke, his voice was intense but low.

"Let me tell you a story."

Chapter 20

"You said he quit racing. You're right, he did, but not because I beat him at the Trials," Eagle said.

He seemed to take a moment to collect his memories and, bobbing his head to the side as if he'd made a decision, continued talking, louder now to overcome the noise of the road. He kept his eyes steady, only flicking down to check the gauges.

"Go back before the Trials. You can't understand Rob unless you do. Me either, for that matter." He waited. "We were both the best in our states in high school, me in Montana, him in Colorado. We met once, the last year of the Kinney Cross-Country Championship—before they changed the name to Foot Locker—when we were seniors.

"There was no Internet back then so we kept track of competition by looking up who had done what in *Running Times*. Every month a new digest, every month I'd check to see what the top runners had done, who had whupped me. All the time, I'm checking those times and seeing the same names, month after month during the season. From my sophomore year on, I was tops in the state, but that wasn't good enough. By god, I was going to be the next Billy Mills, 'cept I was going to go to Oregon, where all the running gods went, instead of Kansas.

"I was pretty much an angry jerk back then. There are still a lot of idiots who think that Native Americans can't run, that we're all a bunch of drunks and drug addicts living off the government. It was worse then. Most assholes didn't bother to cover up the fact they were racists when they shouted crap like 'Run, Tonto' and laughed, but I kept training, used that anger to get stronger and faster and beat the white kids every chance I got.

"Mills had class. I never met Billy and I'm not sure I want to. There's something unsettling about meeting a hero and discovering that he's not a god, just a guy, maybe with all the same flaws as the rest of us.

"So, angry kid, and Oregon doesn't offer. Some chump from Colorado, the same damn chump whose name is always next to mine, a spot behind one month, a spot ahead of me, announces he's going to be a Duck. When I finally meet him, at Kinney, he's this all-American boy with the blond hair and tan."

"He hated Oregon," said Becca.

"Yeah, well, served him right," said Eagle, a sarcastic edge to his voice. "Try L.A. For a kid from Montana, it was overwhelming, all those people, everybody in a big damn hurry to go nowhere fast. All I could think about was getting back to my mountains.

"Anyway, we meet at Kinney and it takes me about ten seconds to figure out what's most annoying about Rob."

He glanced at Becca.

"Want to take a guess?"

She shook her head. Joseph stirred beside her. "He is a very good man," he said.

"Yeah, exactly. He's so sincere and gosh-darned nice, not in a kiss-ass way. It's just who he is. Until you get him on the track. Then he'll rip your frickin' head off or kill himself trying. Which I found out when I started talking crap to him at Kinney and he just takes it, smiles and nods.

"Race starts and he bolts out and tries to take the lead, so I follow him out. He knows I'm right there, along with a couple of other guys, including Corey Ihmels, who ended up winning. He went on to run at Iowa State, I think.

"So Ihmels grabs the lead and runs away from us and we lose the front pack, so it's just the two of us and the damn man would not quit. I'd try to get a little surge going and he'd cover everything. He's all lathered up, practically foaming."

He looked over to Becca, his eyes glinting in the green light of the dash.

"You know what it's like, San Diego. It's winter everywhere else and suddenly you show up for the championship and it's eighty degrees out and gorgeous except it's too hot for racing. I'm thinking that your dad is going to go into heat stroke any second and that's when I'll take him. Meantime, my head feels like it's going to explode from the heat.

"Finish is in sight, he's still right there with me and I kick, he goes with me but I got a better kick, not much but just enough so I get to the line like a hundredth of a second ahead of him, which is all I need. At this point, I don't care about the other guys ahead of us, I just want to beat the jerk who stole my spot at Oregon.

"And I did, but before I can start talking more trash, he comes over. We're both still hunched over sucking wind and I'm like this close to puking it all up but he sticks out his hand.

"I look at him like *what the hell?* and grab it.

He shakes it, tells me it was great racing against me. First guy ever to shake my hand at a race."

Eagle paused and sighed, deep in the memories. He drove, unconsciously adjusting speed as the road got rougher. The turnout with the rope bridge appeared, hazy with smoke and lit with a diffused red light from the fire across the river. The stench of burnt wood, seared earth, triggered a coughing attack in Becca.

Ahead, yellow flashing lights crossed the road and Eagle picked up his right foot and the truck began to slow. On the other side of the barrier, flashing strobes on the top of a crew rig parked on the left side of the road showed firefighters in jerky activity.

"This might be a problem," said Eagle. He reached up and grabbed the placard from the top of the dash.

"You two just sit there and don't say a word."

He tapped the brakes and dimmed his lights as they coasted up to the sawhorses supporting a stout wood beam. Attached to the top of the beam were three battery-powered blinking lights with four-inch lenses that would be clearly visible to any approaching vehicles. Hanging from the bottom was a black-and-white sign with ROAD CLOSED written on it.

He rolled down the window and the dust chasing them caught up and infiltrated the cab. One of the men on the work truck dropped down and walked their way while the rest of them finished loading back on board. Eagle stuck his arm out of the cab and waved the placard.

"Just ferrying some supplies down to the next junction," he shouted. "Greenwood gave his okay and the pass." He waved the plastic card again, turning it so that the symbol of the Forest Service was plain to see.

The man stopped and stuck a palm up in acknowledgement. "Okay, but be quick. The wind's blowin' the fire all over the damn county. No tellin' how long till it jumps the breaks."

"Gotcha, I'll keep my ass in gear," the coach said.

The crew chief threw up his palm again and returned at a brisk walk to the truck, jumping up into the passenger seat. Before he had slammed the door, the driver had the wheels rolling.

Becca let out a breath and her chin dropped slightly.

"I didn't think of roadblocks."

"Neither did I," admitted Eagle.

"But you . . . the pass . . ." Becca fumbled with her words as she tried to understand.

The corners of Eagle's eyes crinkled with pleasure.

"I think it's Greenwood's parking pass," he said. "He should lock his car next time. And those guys"—he indicated the taillights all but gone up the mountain road—"got bigger problems than me."

"You *stole* it?"

Eagle's response was quick and biting. "I left him some beads; it's not like it's Manhattan."

Becca shook her head angrily at the rebuke but didn't reply.

Eagle sighed and said, "Sorry, Becca. I'm not an angry jerk anymore, just a recovering one."

He shifted into gear and eased the pickup to the right side of the road. Both sides were clear, since the roadblock sat in the middle. The right tires dropped down to the weeds on the edge of the gravel and then he straightened it up and accelerated. He seemed lost in thought and the silence in the vehicle lent volume to the wind buffeting them on the outside and the pinging ricochets of rock chips popping up into the undercarriage, kicked loose by the tires.

Becca needed sound, a connection, to hold back the worry, to add in some hope.

"What about my dad? Why did he stop?"

"I know you've heard a lot of these stories from your pop, so bear with me.

"It's an eye-opener when you get to college. Seems like everybody was all-state from somewhere and suddenly you're not that special. Plus, moving to a city blew me away. By the end of the first year, I was ready to chuck and leave, go back home. The Pac-10 championships are in Pullman that year. Rob comes up to me while we're standing around after the race—he never would talk before the race, never—he comes up to me and just stands there. He's just kinda looking around and then looks at me and says, "I miss the mountains." And walks away. And I'm thinking, *Yeah, me too.*

"A week later, I get a phone call from him and he invites me down to the Springs to visit for the summer. No warning, just come on down and we'll run. I figure he's a crazy son-a-bitch but, hell, it could be fun.

"Long story short, every summer we train together, first Colorado, then up here, and always in the mountains. All the time, we're both climbing the rankings and we're one, two in the conference, mostly me first. When we graduate, the Olympics are a year away. By now the Kenyans are just dominating everything from the eight hundred meters to the marathon internationally. I tell Rob I'm going to run in the Olympics and he just laughs a little and tells me we'd better get to work."

He glanced at Becca. "Not 'you'd.' *We'd.* So I laugh at him, tell him that he's going to have to go through me to get on the team." He shook his head. "I'm a slow learner. The next day we head out and Rob just bombs up this mountainside, blows it up for twenty, twenty-five hundred feet of climb—and mind you, we're already eight thousand feet above sea level, so it's not like there's any oxygen to start with. I chase him all the way up until we hit this point and he finally stops, all hunched over, puking his guts out. I'm not much better. I tried to call him an asshole, but I couldn't get enough air to talk, so I just give him some space."

The crinkles showed up at the eyes again. "I called him an asshole later." He drifted away into the memories again and Becca heard the plinking of the stones again. Beside her, Joseph was quiet. She wasn't sure if he was awake.

"I wandered off. When I come back a couple minutes later, he's standing there, out on the edge of the point, a thousand-foot drop under him. You could see to forever up there, the air was so crisp and clear.

"Rob doesn't look at me when he starts talking. I'm number six in the country in the 5K, he's eighth. He looked it up in *Running Times*—they had rankings by then—and knew exactly who would be gunning for the team. The qualifying time was a 13:29, faster than our PRs.

"We spent a year training. When the weather got too cold to train, we moved to Arizona, lived out of a beat-up trailer. Your mom and dad were already engaged and she came down with us, cooked while she took some graduate classes. All we did was run. We both had sponsorships, so we had enough money to eat but not much more. Two, three times a day, we'd head out and rack miles. Once a week, we'd hit the track, just enough that our feet didn't forget what it felt like. Mostly, we kept to trails. Rob cleared it with our coach. Coach said it would either work or break us, but we were really young and had more years left to try, so *what the hell?*" Eagle shrugged.

"Three weeks before the Trials, we're back in Colorado for a week of playing in the mountains. The Trials are in Atlanta that year and we're waiting as long as we can before we bake in the humidity.

"First day we arrive, Rob starts that same stupid climb. He doesn't tell me first, just lets me chase him. We hit the top and it hurts but not nearly so bad as I thought it would. Rob's shaking his head, and smilin'.

" *'We got this,'* he says. He shows me his watch and we're like *sixteen minutes* faster on that climb. Sixteen minutes. And we're both standing there, looking out. I'm thinking that if you'd asked us to run around the world, we'd just nod and pack a lunch. We were bulletproof."

He glanced at Becca. She saw it out of the corner of her eye. "You're starting to know that feeling. You run a lot like him, you know. Same smooth glide, no wasted motion. You need a bigger kick."

Becca didn't look at him but nodded. *Keep talking,* she thought. *Why did he quit?* And an uncomfortable feeling inside, *Am I like him that way, too?*

"That was the only time he talked smack to me, up there at the top of the world. He looked me dead in the eye, told me that I'd have to beat him to make the team. It was a real quiet run back to town."

Eagle cleared his voice.

"When we get back, he's checking mail, it's been piling up while we were in Arizona. I knew I had a pile of my own in Missoula but none of that mattered. We were runners and the Olympics were coming so that was about the only thing we thought about.

"He reads a letter and hands it to your mom. She reads it

and looks at him with that serious look of hers. *'What are you going to do,'* she asks, and I'm thinking *What the . . . ?*

"Neither one of them will tell me what's going on. Your dad's pretty close-mouthed. Anyway, we finish up and head for the Trials. Weather sucks, hot and humid as hell even though it's June. We go through the preliminaries and we both qualify for the finals. We knew we would.

"Race time and we both still need qualifying times. We didn't race much getting ready and we've put our eggs into this one race. Gun goes off and so do we. Pace is a bit slow so your dad starts to push the leaders a bit and I follow him out. First mile is a 4:25, so we're a bit behind pace and your dad pushes again. We take turns leading each other, every other lap, working it like a team. We're back on qualifying pace but there's four runners ahead of us.

"Your dad starts his kick six hundred meters out. He's in front and I stick to him like glue. We both know we got to catch three of those guys for both of us to go. Me, I'm thinkin' I need us to catch two 'cuz I'm gonna be able to take your dad on the kick."

His voice trailed off and he was staring into the far distance.

"Almost didn't. Your dad just kept going and it was all I could do to hang with him. All that time blasting up and down the mountain had made him frickin' strong. I didn't realize just how strong until I'm trying to catch him. I'm only a step behind but just not able to close more. We go into the last turn, your pop takes the number-two lane and goes past the guy in third place. I go around him too and then we're heading for the line. I got to the tunnel-vision stage early, could just see the line, hear your dad. I passed him finally about thirty meters out and finish in 13:24, qualifying. Your dad runs 13:24.6, except he's fourth. Second fastest race I ever ran.

"He comes over, shakes my hand again, lot of other people willing to do it now, too, and gives me a hug. Then he disappears."

"This is the part your pop didn't tell you." His voice was low and, uncharacteristically for the coach, sad.

Becca stirred, glancing at him, her forehead wrinkled.

"I get a call from your mom a week later. Remember that letter I told you about?"

Becca nodded.

"It was from a cancer clinic in Portland."

"My dad had cancer?" asked Becca, disbelieving.

"No. But he was a match for someone who did. As a part of the program at Oregon, he submitted a sample to a donor program for bone marrow transplants. The letter told him he was a match for a young lady with leukemia. So, right after the Trials, he jumped on a plane and they did some more testing and set up the surgery.

"It's a pretty safe procedure. They harvest the cells from the back of both hips. They knocked him out to do it and it takes a little bit of time to recover but minimal risk.

"Except he got some kind of infection a couple of days after the surgery. I think it's because his immune system was weak from the training and race, but however it happened, your dad was one sick puppy.

"I flew out when I heard, and visited him. He looked like crap but he's the same old Rob. He's mostly worried that he put off the surgery too long and asks me to check up on the girl. I tell him I will. We make easy talk about training when he gets out of the hospital but we both know it's bullshit. It's going to take months for him to recover. I'm on my own for the Olympics.

"As I'm getting ready to leave, he calls me back over and he starts talking about the Olympics. Looks me dead in the eye...."

Eagle's voice caught as he remembered.

"Looks me in the eye and tells me I'm representing two nations now, to honor them both."

The road started to nose down again, curling back to the river. Three separate rosy glows bled through the smoke and haze, one in front of them, very faint, one off to the right and brighter, and an angry red that pulsed from just behind them, where the rope bridge had been. Eagle scrounged around in the dark before continuing.

"The infection was nasty. When your dad got out of the hospital, he didn't have the same juice as before. He figured it was just a matter of time and healing. Your mom said he'd head out and run, come back in limping. And all the time, he obsessed about the girl. He had put off the transplant until after the Trials. When he found out how sick she really was, he acted like he was guilty of some crime."

"Did the girl die?" Becca could picture her dad, feeling guilty over something that wasn't even his fault. That much hadn't changed in all the intervening years.

Eagle laughed.

"You tell me," he responded. "Sandi look okay to you?"

Becca's mind boggled and she could see Eagle's sardonic smirk in the windshield.

"He asked me to check up on her. Not sure he expected me to marry Sandi, but she's the toughest person I've ever met, the only lady I ever found that could handle this old Indian. The two of them make a pair. She was a student at Oregon and would watch him at Hayward Field. He acts guilty for waiting so long; she's that way because he's never been able to run again, not really. And, in his case, he wonders what he could have done if the infection hadn't whacked him. And that makes him feel guilty, too. "

The coach dumped something in her lap. The radio.

"We've got an angle to the river from here. See if you can get hold of him. If he answers, great. If not, keep talking anyway."

Becca felt in the dark and located the power button. She turned it on and heard static.

"What do I say?"

Eagle was quiet for a minute.

"Tell him the cavalry is riding hard. All he has to do is hang on."

Becca stared at the radio for a second and keyed the mic.

"Daddy, if you can hear this, we're coming." She sniffled and let go of the button, listened, then pressed it again. *"We're coming, Daddy, just hang on. It's not much longer and you can do this. Please don't quit. Uncle Jim and me and Joseph will be there soon. Hang tough, please, Daddy, please hang tough. . . ."*

As her voice broadcast into the air, Jim Eagle wiped a hand across his eyes.

Chapter 21

Becca wrinkled her nose. Something in the dark nearby had died, and the stench carried on the gusting wind, mixed with the charred smell, full of bitter pine sap, from the burnt lodge-poles. The space to the trees surrounding the trailhead was filled with acrid haze and her throat was already protesting. She heard the engines of a plane overhead but couldn't tell if it was another spotter plane or an air tanker called in to drop water on the flames.

Eagle was getting water out of the bed of the pickup, the rear light a bright white halo that faded to gray at the edges. He turned, the bluish sweep of his LED headlamp showing the gravel of the parking area for the trailhead, paused briefly on the signage on the wood posts, and settled on her and Joseph, blinding them. He clicked off his light, squinting into theirs. Becca turned her head to direct her light away but didn't turn it off.

"Here's the plan. Becca, I want you leading us out. Walk the first bit until your legs loosen up. And keep the pace down, not more than a slow jog." A nugget of worry settled into her stomach but they were finally, finally, finally going. It calmed her mind but not her stomach. Cinching the straps on the run pack didn't either, but action, any action, moved her one step closer.

Eagle saw the impatience and turned to face her.

"I mean it. You've already covered a bunch of miles today. It's seventeen miles from here to the spot where your dad splashed in, so you're looking at marathon-type distances. This isn't a race, it's a rescue mission, and we can't do crap if we get there fried. Got it?"

Becca dropped her eyes as a gust of wind rocked her. She leaned into the gust until it faded.

"Uh-huh."

"Okay." He paused. "Joseph, you're right behind her until we all get warmed up, then take the lead. Don't outrun us. The trail gets a bit rougher and overgrown a couple of miles up and I want you clearing some of it for Becca."

Joseph's headlight bounced up and down in agreement. His hands were busy with his pack, a heavier system with more water and storage than Becca's. He was their "mule," the strong guy that carried all the extra supplies to let the others run without expending excess energy.

"We've got four hours to dawn. That will get us close to the far end. We might miss him on the way out in the dark but, if we do, we'll catch him when we double back."

He walked back to the truck and slammed the door shut and the light over the bed went out. The smoke closed in around her headlight, emitting the same blue of the others. The ground in front of her was distorted by the light, flat and missing the richness of definition she was used to in a three-dimensional world. As she tilted her head, the beam lit the entrance to the trail, a gap in the trees. The wind beat at the tops of the trees. Pops and creaks from the swaying branches competed with the river rushing past on her left.

She walked forward and watched the others fall in behind her, the shadows cast by their lights reaching past her. They were nearly silent as they tracked her.

The leaves of the plants held an unhealthy tinge and the movement of the shadows disoriented her. She lowered her head to see where she was stepping and focused on that. The distortions didn't change. The ground looked flat and unvarying but she could feel the divots and small rocks under her feet. Her feet picked up speed and she recognized, more by feel, that she was headed slightly downhill. Her eyes couldn't see the slope of the ground and all the soil looked the same except for the largest rocks and branches.

She ducked abruptly as something came at her from the right, near her head. It grabbed her hair and then she was past.

A branch, she thought, as she came back upright. *Need to look up, too.*

Becca grunted as she broke into a slow jog using the downhill. She kept her feet low and her stride short while her body loosened up. A toe scuffed the dirt when the trail rose and her stomach lurched as she stumbled slightly. Becca straightened, and her stride got longer as the muscles warmed.

Somewhere ahead was her dad, and she wondered if he had his headlight in the pack he carried. A spark of fear arced and faded.

Probably, she thought, reassured, but to the sides all she could see was black, and in front was the weirdly lit trail and more black. Becca pictured her dad out here without light and her breathing picked up to the point that she was panting.

"Breathe, Rebecca," came Joseph's voice behind her. "We are here with you."

The sound of his voice was comforting. She took the incipient fear and placed it into a box and set it aside in a corner of her mind, just as she had been taught. She could hear her dad's voice, from when she was nine or ten. *"You own the inside of your head."* He had showed her how to get focused on racing, seeing the outcome before it happened, visualizing each step of the course until she finished.

Now Becca projected up the trail. The slow run followed the meander of the river as it wound through the canyon. There were some ups and downs, never big at the bottom of the valley floor like this. Blurring the projection was the dream she'd had in the truck. She saw him clear of the river, on his way toward them. He was walking, not running, but moving. Alive.

As she watched in her mind, he stumbled and fell. She tried to will him to get up, keep moving, but the image was fading away, the blackness around her surrounding him. His body became indistinct and was gone. She couldn't feel him out there anymore.

"Becca?"

Eagle's concerned voice connected and brought her back to the present. She was standing still on the trail, staring at her feet. The wind in the trees was loud. She hadn't noticed the wind picking up behind them.

"You okay?"

"What if we don't find him?"

"I don't buy trouble before I have to," said Eagle. His voice was soft. "Right now, we just worry about what we can do. And if you can't go, we need to turn back right now because I'm not losing you *and* him."

She gave a shake of her head and the light played over her trail shoes. They were nearly the same color as the dirt.

"I'm okay."

"I will lead now," said Joseph. A quiet declarative sentence, but the undertones carried worry and compassion.

Becca didn't answer and Joseph stepped past her. She turned and waited for him to get a few feet ahead and began to tread behind him.

The young Kenyan ran softly, his feet almost caressing the earth. He carried his hands higher than she did, the palms up toward his chest with little wasted motion at the elbows. He had powerful thighs and the fine-boned calves and wrists that marked him as a member of the Kalenjin tribe at home. He didn't so much run as flow effortlessly over the ground.

His stride was surprisingly short, and it took a second to comprehend how much he was slowing down for her.

The sound of an alarm from Eagle's watch violated the quiet of the night.

"Walk break," he said from behind, and they each eased to a brisk walk.

Becca reached for her water bottle. Joseph was sucking on the bite valve of his water bladder. She spun the pack around her waist to unzip it. She took out an energy bar.

"Share?" she asked as she tore the wrapper open along the seam.

"I'm good," said Eagle.

"Yes, please," said Joseph.

She handed over half of the cookies-and-cream-flavored bar. The strong gusts of wind ruffled her clothes as she munched on the bar. It was nearly tasteless in the smoky air. Becca stuffed the wrapper into a pocket.

"Time," declared Eagle.

They had been running two or three minutes when they came across the first downed tree lying across the trail, dead limbs extended over the river. One at a time, they clambered over it. Becca winced as she scratched the inside of her thigh on the rough bark.

Joseph took the lead again and Becca dropped into the easy pace that he set. She was nearly up to speed when pain exploded in her left foot, and she was windmilling through the air, arms flailing for something to grab hold of, but there was only open space, a split second of comprehension that she was falling, followed by the hammering impact to the ground.

Chapter 22

Becca stared at the headlamp as the stars in her head faded.
Impact with the ground had flung the light ahead of her but the
tough LEDs survived the shock. Now the beam shot off toward
the river three feet past her, casting long shadows from each
tiny pebble and twig it crossed. Little dust motes were resettling
to earth as she took a deep, trembling breath, her body twitchy.

"You okay?"

Strong hands reached down and grasped her under her
armpits. Becca felt herself lifted off the ground effortlessly as
Jim Eagle set her on her feet. Joseph doubled back to them. He
stooped to pick up the light.

She nodded dumbly while she took inventory. Nothing hurt
horribly, so nothing broken. Left foot throbbing. She must have
broken her fall with her left arm because the shoulder, already
sore from the river, was crying for attention. A glance at her
hand confirmed some cuts, blood just beginning to well out

around little black clumps of dirt. Same thing on one knee. Seeing it opened the pathway from the damaged skin to her brain. It added its signals to those from the other abused parts.

Both the men were taking the same inventory, from the outside instead of the inside. Joseph reached out his right hand to brush away twigs stuck to her sweat but it left a streak of mud.

"Sorry," she said, adjusting the light back onto her head. *Pick up your feet, dummy,* she thought to herself.

"It happens to all of us," said Eagle.

"Perhaps," said Joseph.

Becca shot him a skeptical look and saw him shrug, lips twisted in a wry hint of a smile. She ignored him and his smile widened another millimeter.

Turning to Eagle, she asked, "Do we have enough water I can rinse these a bit?"

"Quickly," he said. "We're on a time goal."

She winced when the water sluiced across the scrapes. She used the bandana to pat the cuts dry. Joseph handed her a couple of Band-Aids, the wrappers already open. She put them on the worst of the wounds. The rest would be okay, she decided.

While she was tending to herself, Eagle was looking west with a frown.

Becca looked to the horizon. Low against the sky was an orange-tinged glow that penetrated the overlying reef of smoke above them. Her nose must have gone dead, because she couldn't smell the smoke anymore.

"That wasn't there when we left." She made the statement a question.

"The wind is pushing it hard," said Eagle. He peered into the dark, trying to measure time and distance. "We're gonna have to pick it up."

While he spoke, Becca turned and put the headlamp on. The band was wet where she had splashed some water on it to wash off the dirt. She cinched the band tight and adjusted the beam to the ground.

"Let's roll," said Becca. Before either of the men could react, she was ahead of them on the trail. In the dark, they couldn't see her grimace with the first couple of steps as the left foot hit the ground. She must have jammed something. She modified her stride to take some of the pressure off the big toe. That helped.

"You are very bossy tonight," said Joseph quietly, as he slipped past to take the point.

Becca concentrated on protecting the battered digit and getting her feet up so she wouldn't fall again. The disorientation she felt from the movement of the light and the weirdness of the shadows slowly faded as her brain adapted to the new information. She still had a problem on descents with measuring the steepness, so she slowed on them, landing on her heels.

Uphills hurt, hurt bad, every time she would toe off with the left foot. There was no way to compensate so she mentally gritted her teeth and forced her foot through its normal range of motion. The uphills were short but she would hit the top panting.

Eagle finally called another walking break. As Becca stumbled to a walk, Eagle came up behind her and spoke in her left ear.

"You're limping."

She waited, expecting him to tell her to turn around. She wouldn't be able to wheedle him out here, but he couldn't carry her back, either.

"Go on ahead. I'm slowing you down." The rasp was back in her throat. Even if she couldn't smell it, the smoke was still doing its damage. A dull pain was building behind her eyes.

"No," said Joseph. "We do not leave pretty young women in the woods by themselves."

Becca blushed in the dark, oddly pleased at the flirt.

A light chuckle came from behind her.

"Ever seen a movie where the heroes abandon the girl?" asked Eagle, joining them.

"This isn't a movie," said Becca.

"True, but we got the pretty girl, as the sidekick there noted, and we're on a desperate mission to save a comrade. Sounds like a movie to me." He laughed again. "That makes me the hero, of course."

Becca shook her head as she walked.

"Eat something," said Eagle, "not too much though. Then we'll get restarted—*together.*"

Becca's fingers were swollen and clumsy but she found an energy bar. She ripped open the wrapper with her teeth, releasing the scent of apples and cinnamon, and took a bite. She wolfed half of it in three bites while they walked. She washed each bite down with water. She covered up the remainder and put it away for later. Rustles in the dark told her the two men were doing the same.

"How far have we gone?" Becca asked. The dark robbed her of any way of estimating distance. Her watch said they had been running for almost ninety minutes. In daylight, rested, she would have covered a dozen miles, but all her frames of reference, even the way her body felt, were messed up. Her thighs ached, a deep heaviness as the miles piled up and the foot sent continuous messages of abuse. Even her hair hurt.

"About eight miles, I think. We're making good time."

Becca did the math in her head, came out with a ridiculous number, and tried again. It wasn't just her body that was tired.

"Eleven-minute miles?"

Jim Eagle confirmed it. " 'Bout that. For night running, pretty good."

"It is time," said Joseph. He switched from a quick walk to a slow jog so smoothly that he was ten yards ahead of them before Becca got started.

She closed up on him, leaving enough room to see obstructions and dodge them. The energy bar sat like a brick in her stomach. Occasionally she'd burp and taste the cinnamon again, mixed with stomach acid. She reached for her water bottle and rinsed her mouth while she ran, careful to watch her footing.

Her eyes strained to make out the variations in the running surface. In front, she could see Joseph's light—though not Joseph except when she shifted her light up. From behind her, Eagle's headlamp would dance up to her feet, changing the angles and patterns in a flashing black and blue-white kaleidoscope. She twisted her neck and some of the stress relaxed, but only temporarily.

Joseph's light ducked unexpectedly and he called "*brahnch*" with the soft vowel to warn her to duck but she only dipped her head an inch and was past it. Once, Joseph abruptly stopped, waving his arms. He plucked at his face, his features twisting into a grimace.

"Spider web," he explained.

Becca was glad that he was leading.

She felt herself getting sleepy and then she yawned, surprising herself. She stumbled slightly mid-yawn, which drew a quick "Okay?" from Eagle behind her.

She lifted her right hand in a lazy wave that she wasn't sure he'd see.

"Yeah," she said over her shoulder and yawned again. She kept her head moving, looking for some sign of her dad. The longer they ran, the more unsettled the night became. She held the worry away from her like it was a separate being, with a life of its own that could, for now, be ignored. Ignored or not, it wormed its way into her attention whenever she let her mind wander.

The trail curved away from the river and the steady noise of the water against the shore faded into the night. As they hit a bend, Becca saw a pair of silent silvery eyes reflecting her light back, watching them as the rescue party ran past. A second pair joined them, and then the animals must have turned their heads and the eyes vanished. Becca hadn't seen enough to gauge the size of the animal or type. Her skin crawled. In the dark, she couldn't tell if they were deer or wolves. The little hairs on the back of her neck stayed prickled for the next mile as she cast nervous glances to the sides as she ran.

Neither man acted as though he had seen anything. They powered on smoothly and steadily. Becca matched them for pace but her stride felt forced and choppy. She could feel the strain in her knees and, with the observation, the skinned shin clamored for its share of her attention. She shook it off and focused but her brain meandered around, dragging out, like faded pictures, old crashes to compare against. All the meanders led to her mom or dad picking her up, patching her up, and making the encouraging sounds parents were expected to say. She missed the reassurances.

The memories were broken up when they took another walking break, and Becca shivered as the sweat started to dry. They had shivered through several microclimates already, small bubbles of cold air that lasted for a few steps up to a couple hundred yards, each shocking the skin at the five or ten degrees' difference in the air temperature. She had thought repeatedly about the long pants she had left in the truck, a twinge of regret each time at leaving them there.

This was different though, she thought. A glance at her watch confirmed that dawn was only an hour away. She looked ahead but either the trees were blocking the first blushes of dawn or it was too early. She looked behind her and the ruddy glow was still there. Maybe bigger. She would have traded sides for the glow in a heartbeat, she thought with a knot in her stomach. Much, much better from the east.

Fourteen miles, she thought, then: *We missed him.*

No one said anything, but Eagle and Joseph were both more alert now that they were in the vicinity of where they expected to find Hawthorne. Birds, the earliest risers, were beginning their morning song. At home, she would lie and listen to them before getting up for a morning run, but today, the gaiety of the warbles passed by her unappreciated as she trudged forward.

Her foot ached but it seemed to be steady rather than worsening. The pain behind her eyes was getting sharper and her throat felt swollen from breathing the crappy air.

Joseph looked back. She squeezed her eyes shut as his light blinded her, leaving a dancing pattern scattered on the inside of her eyelids.

"Time, again," he said, and turned forward, moving into that efficient low-speed jog he was using.

Eyes still closed while they recovered, Becca heard something—more like a lack of something. The bird calls changed. To her left, the calls had disappeared. Her head twitched that way, eyes still clenched tightly and heart thumping. She willed it to thump quietly but it banged and echoed in her ears.

Jim Eagle put a hand in the small of her back.

"Let's go, Becca," he said gently.

She jerked her chin sideways an inch and the hand disappeared.

". . . -becca . . ."

Her head snapped to face the word, so faint that she caught herself praying that it was real as she opened her eyes to the hazy dark, the beam of her light casting crazy shadows from the trunks of the pines that receded into a dense patch of darkness.

Eagle's light joined hers.

"Becca?" His voice was cautious.

She heard Joseph turning back as she left the trail, pushing through the low plants along the side. One step, and listen hard, harder than she had ever listened, enough to make jaws hurt from the tension.

Just the birds to the sides, and the river chugging around some rocks, unseen in the night, and her heart, pounding . . . and nothing else.

She took another step, and another. The patch of darkness resolved itself into dense brush, thick and man-high, twenty feet away.

". . .—ca-bear . . ."

"Dad?"

Behind her, she heard Joseph and Eagle enter the woods on either side of her, swinging wide to form a search line without thinking, spaced about five yards away from Becca.

Louder this time, and now they all heard it; not a word, just the moan and the thrashing of a man trying to get to his feet.

Becca broke to the right, Joseph's side, as they hurriedly circled around the foliage, forcing their way through the edges where it was penetrable. Eagle got there first.

"Oh, holy shit," he said, overwhelmed. "Oh, hell."

Becca was only a second behind him from the other side, forcing her way past Joseph.

She gasped as her eyes widened. Becca almost didn't recognize the man as her father.

Chapter 23

All Becca could see was dried blood on a body that looked as though it had been through a threshing machine. Eagle and Joseph sped to her father's side while she stood gaping, a painful lump in her chest.

Instead of skirting the edge of the dense thicket, Rob Hawthorne had tried to force his way through and was wedged into the branches, knees not even touching the ground, almost as though he had laid down face-first into a thorny hammock. As she watched, he feebly moved his feet, toes scratching spastically at the hard dirt as he tried to push forward. A soft moan drifted from him.

"...-bear?"

He was shirtless and one shoe was missing. A pair of massive bruises showed on his back, wickedly livid and raised. The larger one, high on the left shoulder blade, was still seeping blood where the skin was split. The blood looked black in the light of their LEDs, and it glistened. Small rivulets dripped down his body, a dozen small cuts that had crusted over. As he flung his head slowly side to side, she saw a cut over his eye, the left one, closest to her, and more bruises on his dirty face. He had fallen, clearly more than once, and some of the dirt was attached in the crusted blood. His eyelid was sealed shut.

Her dad's voice was an exhausted whisper, from a man forced past whatever limits he thought he had, and filled with torment and agony. Yet, it carried a heartbreakingly thin reed of hope, too. He turned his head to try to see her, effort made of sheer will and determination.

The sound of his voice galvanized her into action. She rushed to his side. As she came closer, she saw that he had splinted the fractured bone, and her eyes grew wide as she imagined setting a broken arm with no help.

The splint was built from sticks, crudely held in position by what was left of his shirt, and the whole thing was tied with a shoelace. The fragments of shirt were splotched and blackened with the ends of the broken braces extending past the elbow. His run pack was hanging from his neck and Becca saw that he had used it as a sling. The zipper was open and the pack was empty.

Eagle got there first and dropped to a knee as he shrugged off his pack. He reached out to place a hand on Rob's back.

Eagle spoke gently. "Easy, brother, easy."

Becca knelt on the other side of her father.

She reached out a hand too but hesitated, uncertain where to touch her father, not wanting to cause him more pain. She dropped her arm back to her side.

Eagle looked over Hawthorne's back at Becca.

"Keep talking to him but try to keep him from moving," he said to Becca.

Becca began talking to her dad, softly and low.

"We're here, Daddy," she whispered around clenched jaws as tears formed. "We're all here. It's going to be okay."

She hoped that he couldn't hear the quiver in her voice, the fear. She didn't know what else to say so she kept repeating the same platitudes, hoping that the words wouldn't obscure the meaning.

Eagle glanced up to Joseph, who was already pulling a first-aid kit and extra bandages from his backpack.

"We need two long poles. I've got a camp saw in my bag," he said, reaching behind him and tossing the bag at the other man. "Dig it out. They need to be mostly straight, about seven feet long—make it eight—and not too thick around for us to hang on to."

Joseph handed over the medical wipes and nodded as he began measuring all the nearby saplings.

"I will find some."

Becca kept talking to Rob as Eagle dug around in his bag. She knew she was babbling but she forced herself to keep talking. As her dad calmed and stopped struggling, she put a hand on his shoulder.

A few yards away, she could hear Joseph start on the first sapling, the *shoup, shoup* of the saw blade biting wood as regular as a metronome in the dark.

"This is going to stick a bit," said Eagle inanely to the injured man.

Becca looked at the coach. He had a syringe in his hand, loaded with an ampule of yellowish liquid. He rubbed a spot on Rob's arm and jammed the syringe in, depressing the plunger. The ampule broke, the tinkling musical sound out of place, and the fluid disappeared into Rob.

"What was that?"

Eagle didn't answer her. He wrapped up the used device in a wet wipe and rubbed it thoroughly until the packaging, the tube, and all the parts were wetted.

"What did you give my dad?" The words came out way harder than she meant.

Eagle stood up with the bundle in his hand.

"Morphine."

She looked at him, stunned. *Morphine?* Her eyes darted around as she tried to figure it out. Not why he had given her dad the opiate, but where he had gotten it from.

"Watch his breathing. I'll be right back."

Seconds later, she heard him scuffing at the dirt as he buried the evidence. He came back, wiping his palms on his shorts.

"Where did you get morphine from?" She kept control of her voice this time. She already suspected the answer and she tried to picture herself taking that big a risk. She couldn't, her mind boggled at the idea, but it was accompanied by a subtle tinge of guilt. What she couldn't imagine, Eagle had done.

For *her* dad.

A crack announced the felling of a small tree and Eagle glanced that way.

"Keep talking to him, but let's get him out of the weeds. Once Joseph cuts the poles, we'll build a stretcher—I was half-hopin' he'd be able to walk, but we're going to have to carry him out."

He knelt again beside Rob and shot a look over to Becca.

"Ready?"

"Yeah."

"Rob," said Eagle, low and intense, "we're going to ease you back. I need you to let us help you sit down, but wait until we're ready. Do you understand?"

A groan and a small bowing of the neck, like he was too tired to hold up his head. Rob relaxed his legs and Eagle wrapped one sinewy arm around the man's hips. The other went to the back of Rob's upper arm. The coach braced his back leg to take the strain. Becca copied him, right arm crossing Eagle's left, toes of her foot touching his. She didn't grasp his arm, trying to stay away from the break. Instead, she put her hand under his thigh as they built a cradle with their arms.

"Okay, hoss."

Rob lifted his head and, with another drawn-out moan, settled back, first to his haunches, then to a sitting position. His broken arm folded into his lap. In his right hand, Becca saw his radio, clenched tight in his fist.

"Drink?" Hawthorne's voice was a whisper, but she thought he sounded stronger.

Becca kept her right arm around him as she reached with the other to get a bottle. She pulled the valve open with her teeth and held it up to her dad's mouth. As it touched the corner of his lips, he turned his face and opened his mouth a fraction, enough for her to pour water in. She squeezed the bottle to keep a steady flow but on the third gulp he gagged and coughed. She watched as his body twisted, racked with pain.

"Sorry," she said, but he was rocking his head in forgiveness.

Behind her, another tree surrendered to Joseph and the saw.

Eagle was carefully cleaning the gashes on Rob's back. The contents of the first-aid kit were strewn around him and he worked quickly. Rob barely flinched at the ministrations. Once the wounds were clean, he applied an antibiotic ointment and taped squares of white gauze over them.

Becca offered him more water and her dad drank eagerly. The water came faster than he could swallow and the excess dribbled from his chin. There was no way that he could see her, she thought. The cut over his eye looked wicked and the bruising covered most of the left side of his face. She saw him try to force his eye open, the muscles pulling at the dried blood. He yelped and gave up.

"Wait for Uncle Jim," Becca told him. "We'll get it cleaned up."

Eagle checked his handiwork on Rob's back. The bandages stood in stark contrast to the grime on the tanned skin.

"I ain't Florence Nightingale but it'll work until we can get you to a doc," he said. He turned his attention to Rob's face. "Let's get this cleaned up."

Eagle used liberal amounts of water to soften the dried blood and patiently, and very gently, wiped Rob's face.

"Arm . . . broken."

"Yeah, we know. Not much we can do until we get you out of here."

Rob bowed his head and Eagle shifted his body so he could keep working with the water and cloth. Once he had Rob's face clean, he broke out a tube. He snipped the tip off it and squeezed until a bead of viscous liquid appeared. He reached over Rob and applied it to the gash over Rob's eye, lining the edges of the wound.

"This might hurt," he said as he used his fingers to pinch the wound closed. Rob made an *uhh* sound but didn't try to pull away. Eagle let go of the folds of the skin. They stuck together. He quickly put together a bandage and taped it over the sealed injury, trimming a corner so that it wouldn't block Rob's eye.

Becca held up the water bottle again, and her father drank more.

"Thanks," he said, and his voice was noticeably stronger. He looked confused and tried to shift toward his good arm like he was going to stand. As he leaned into the radio he still held, his other arm slid across his lap and he went rigid. He settled back and his shoulders drooped.

Becca pulled out the half of the energy bar she had saved.

"Eat," she instructed.

She broke a small piece of the bar off and held it to his lips. He took it and chewed slowly. When Rob was done chewing, Becca offered him more water.

Eagle gave her a look of approval. He stood up as Joseph returned, dragging two sapling boles, each about three inches in diameter. The two of them stripped the branches off.

"Cut them down some," said Eagle, pointing to the ten-foot lengths. "Then use the leftover to make some cross-braces. We've got plenty of rope to lash it together and we'll use our shirts to fill out the middle. Wind some of the tape around the ends, too."

While the men built the rough stretcher, Becca alternated giving her dad food and water. She could see that Rob's eyes were constricted and a little dazed. *The morphine,* she thought, but he didn't seem to hurt as bad. While his movements were lethargic, they were also purposeful. Becca allowed herself a small measure of hope, the first since the log had smashed into her father. She sat on her haunches as she fed him the last bite of food, as the hours of desperation faded. Hope, even in such a miniscule amount, tingling with renewed energy.

"Okay, we're ready," said Eagle.

Quickly they loaded a protesting Rob—he insisted feebly he could walk—and turned toward the west where the truck waited.

Eagle took the front end and Joseph the back, each hanging on to the ends of the poles, Rob suspended between them.

Becca led, scrambling ahead to move branches out of the way. She glanced behind them, to the east. It was black.

The horizon in front, to the west, was a dull orange, the fire of a fake dawn.

Chapter 24

Beep, beep, beep.

Becca had lost count of the number of times the watch had gone off. They were making frustratingly slow progress, but Eagle insisted on regular rest breaks. He had set his watch to help measure the time, five minutes of carrying followed by two minutes of rest. Joseph set his end of the stretcher down and rolled his shoulders. The river was right next to them. It was a black ribbon in the night, wider here and seeming placid.

Becca had volunteered to help with carrying the stretcher, but both men had rejected the idea.

"Just clear the branches and crap out of our way," Eagle said. It sounded easier than it was. Both men were missing their shirts, donated to help create the stretcher. Both bore small scratches across their chests and shoulders from branches she'd missed.

Becca would hurry to get in front of them and hold the branches back or shift obstructions at ground level. She'd hold position until they were past, and then have to make her way in front. She had finally borrowed the saw from Eagle and began to hack the offending limbs out of the way.

She found a log to sit on to take the weight off her feet. The one that she'd banged was throbbing and both of them were sore.

"How far have we gone?" she asked.

"I figure about a mile and a half," said Eagle. He glanced at his watch. "We should be back to the truck by ten a.m."

The watch twittered again and all three stood up without thinking. It reminded Becca of a lesson in psychology she had semi-snoozed through last year. Something about dogs and bells, she thought. *Pavlov,* she thought, remembering.

Rob was dozing fitfully. He'd given up protesting at being carried. After the second wrenching cry as his broken arm slipped off his chest, Joseph had tied the arm to the rail on the other side of his body. They picked up and put down the stretcher carefully, trying to avoid jarring Hawthorne.

Becca took the lead, her head down as she checked for loose rocks or roots that might trip the guys. She swept a fist-size stone out of the way with the outer edge of her right foot. The clatter of the rock bouncing down to the river was loud in a silent forest. The wind had temporarily died down so even the trees lost their song. Becca had never heard the forest when it was this quiet.

She yawned hugely and had to stop walking until she was done squinting her eyes from it. She looked at her own watch, pressing the button that illuminated the screen.

Four a.m.

Another yawn as she cleared a thin branch, snapping it with her fingers rather than using the saw.

She had been up for nearly a full day, waking just after dawn yesterday. Now another dawn was coming. She glanced back over the river and could see a line of light to the east. The glow to the west hadn't gotten bigger and maybe had even shrunk a bit. She had a hard time focusing on it.

Eagle's watch sounded and she stopped walking. There was no place to sit so she stood there shifting from one tender foot to the other.

"When was the last time you ate something?" asked Eagle.

Becca shrugged. She wasn't hungry, but she didn't argue. She unzipped her pack, found another bar, and ripped open the packaging with a sigh. Her stomach rebelled at the smell and taste, but she forced herself to eat half of it.

"Eggs would be good," she said. "And bacon."

"And coffee," added Joseph, with a smile. "I like coffee with breakfast."

Becca's stomach grumbled as she washed the energy bar down with the last of her water. She eyed the embankment to the river. The ground fell gradually to the inky water.

"Who else needs water? I'm out."

"I'm good," said Eagle.

She eased down to the edge of the water, careful on the slope. She was still having trouble figuring out her footing. She looked for the far bank of the river. She could make out the trees on the other side but the stars were lost in the low-hanging haze from the fire. A fog from the inky surface of the water writhed and twisted in the beam of her headlight. It was eerily quiet. The vapor solidified into spectral and menacing shapes before it dissolved in a sudden gust of wind.

Becca shivered.

She squatted down to reach the water and unscrewed the cap off one of her bottles. She dipped it into the water, extending out as far as her arm would reach, trying to avoid any brackish water that might linger along the bank. She knew from experience that the water in the current would be fresher and healthier. The bottle made popping sounds as the air fled and the water filled. She replaced the top and repeated the process with her other bottle.

Becca heard Eagle's watch chime again and she climbed back to rejoin him and Joseph.

The men were already moving up the trail and headed uphill, too. They had reached the section that swerved away from the river.

"I'm coming," she said after them as she adjusted her gear. Joseph gave a head bob to say that he had heard. She started to jog, stiff-legged and on her heels a bit. It only took her a few seconds to catch up.

"If you let me up front, I'll clear out the crap."

"Doin' okay," said Eagle. The strain of carrying the litter with Rob in it showed in his voice. The usual banter, lighthearted and cheerful, was replaced with . . . *what*? Becca thought about it as she followed. It wasn't angry or fearful or like he was in pain. She watched Joseph, moving steadily, almost feeling ahead with his feet, unable to see through the stretcher. The weight of her father was sitting heavy in Joseph's hands and arms as the two men trudged up the hill.

Determination.

She could tell that they were tired; they were all tired. Becca felt beat to hell, legs as tired as she had ever experienced. Everything hurt, all the way down to her hair follicles. But they didn't complain. And they were carrying her dad. Rob wasn't a big man but it was dead weight. If she had stuck to her original plan to get her dad back without Joseph and Uncle Jim, she would never have made it.

And neither would her dad.

The trail widened as it weaved through the lodgepole pines, and Becca grabbed the opportunity to get out in front of the party just as Eagle's watch signaled the next rest break.

It took them three more breaks before they reached the top of the incline and headed down.

She realized that she could see into the woods on either side. The sun, ever reliable, was gradually lighting the woods as dawn approached. The canopy was shrouded in gray, clinging smoke. She sniffed but still couldn't smell it. Behind her, she heard a clatter of rocks. Becca half turned to see Eagle, his face covered in sweat and dust, the muscles in his arms and chest showing the effort of recovering his balance. Joseph, more compact, had veins popping but betrayed no expression on his face while he struggled to help balance the makeshift stretcher.

Joseph saw her looking at him and he directed a slim smile toward her. The expression touched his eyes in a way that was both friendly and oddly intimate. She flushed and felt like a peeping tom.

They reached the bottom without any further incidents.

Halfway, Becca thought, as the stretcher was laid on the ground. It was encouraging. They weren't covering distance fast but they were making steady progress.

Rob stirred and his eyes opened but they closed again. She watched the rise and fall of his chest, the breaths coming slower than she had ever seen. It seemed impossible for him to get enough air. She was used to slow respiration rates—she was a runner, after all—but this scared her a bit and she counted, *in, out. Nine a minute.*

She sat down on a rock next to him. Her lower back was tight and she bent at the waist to relax it, twisting both ways.

Rob moaned and said something in his drugged sleep but Becca couldn't understand the slurred and mumbled words. His eyes, behind the lids, were jerking.

"Time to take a longer break, folks," said Eagle. He sounded worn. He sucked on the bite valve of his water bag and pulled out yet another energy bar. He held it, weighing it, and then tore it open and took a bite, his face registering his distaste.

A lonesome bird warbled and waited for an answer. It was the first bird that Becca had heard in an hour and the sound stood out in the lonely forest that should have been alive with birds, chirping, cheeping, warbling, and cooing. Just one lonely bird, calling out for company in the morning song.

Joseph kept rolling his shoulders, forward and backward, and did some arm swings, trying to stay loose. White streaks of dried sweat streaked his face along the cheekbones. He gnawed on food.

They sat through an entire cycle of beeps. Becca resisted the impulse to stand on the first round of sound, listened to the second "rest" tune, and rose painfully on the next one. The men stooped and lifted and the troop began trekking to the trailhead.

Six miles? thought Becca with a head that felt stuffed with mush. Three hours. They were moving faster with daylight, even with a weak sun that barely made it to the ground. Everything was unfamiliar despite having traversed the same ground just a few hours ago. Branches were less grabby and the trail smoother, but the smoke was thicker, or at least it seemed thicker.

Twenty-eight minutes later, four cycles of the watch, a new sound reached them. High above them, hidden by the smoke, a plane circled. Becca tracked it by sound. As it completed a second lap, Becca heard another sound, familiar and frightening, close to her feet.

"SNAKE!" she yelled, and she instinctively leapt away from the buzz as her heart accelerated to a hard gallop. She landed six feet away and frantically searched around her in case there was a second snake.

Idiot! she thought, panting, as her wide eyes finished surveying the ground. She knew better than to let her attention wander. *Idiot, idiot, idiot.*

Both men stopped short, Eagle balancing against the crossbar that hit him in the back. He leaned ahead but didn't put another foot forward. Joseph was a half step slower at reacting but pulled back on the poles to help Eagle with his balance.

Between them and Becca lay a rattlesnake, curled into a defensive figure eight. The large head swayed side to side, seeking the source of the threat, but all of them maintained a safe, if uneasy, distance. The tongue slithered out as the snake tried to locate them by taste and smell. Becca knew they were too far away for the snake to find them by temperature—rattlesnakes were pit vipers with heat-seeking receptors—and the eyes were better at night. She stood very, very still and didn't breathe, though the latter was an unconscious reaction.

The rattler had disguised himself against a rock where the trail narrowed, the browns and tans blending into the ground. He was thick but probably not more than four or five feet long, definitely a granddaddy judging by the length of the rattle at the end of his tail. The snake was clearly offended by the lack of respect that Becca had shown by nearly stepping on him, but the tail had stopped its evil buzz. Gradually, the old man snake relaxed, and sinuously reversed his body over itself to disappear into the forest, and Becca breathed again.

"Sorry."

A smile broke out on Eagle's face, the first that she'd seen since they had found her dad. It broadened and his eyes glinted.

"First rule of the trail, Becca—the rattlesnake *always* has right of way," he said.

"Yeah, I know." She glanced skyward but the plane seemed to be gone. "I got distracted."

"We can only carry one of you at a time," said Eagle, "but we'd come back for you."

Becca tried to glare at him but a case of the giggles overwhelmed her. A nervous reaction now that the threat was gone.

Eagle's watch went off and once again they settled the injured man on the ground. Joseph was flexing his hands and she could see that the palms were raw from handling the rough wood. He saw the look and smiled.

"We are nearly there."

She nodded that she understood. They'd worry about themselves soon, once they had Rob out safely and headed for help.

It was on a short rocky downhill that they started to worry about themselves. That's when a rock slid out from under Jim Eagle's foot, twisting his knee, and sent him tumbling, flipping the stretcher on its side. Rob woke with a shriek as his injured arm twisted where it was tied to the stretcher. Joseph fought to keep Rob from falling and two of the crossbars broke free.

Eagle hit the ground hard and started cursing low and mean. His features were twisted in a snarl as he grabbed at his leg.

Becca, horrified, watched a pool of dark, rich blood grow under the right leg of the coach.

Chapter 25

Becca rushed to Eagle. She heard Joseph talking to her dad as he lowered his end of the litter and unlashed the rope that anchored Rob's arm to the pole. She spared a glance at them as she crossed the gap to the other coach in three quick strides, the ache and weariness temporarily dispelled.

Eagle was still cursing inventively as he shifted his weight to his left hip. He favored his right leg, moving it carefully. As it rotated into Becca's view, she gasped.

The skin and flesh were torn just below the kneecap in the meaty part of the shin. A large triangular flap hung down, specked with black, and oozing blood. The tibia, the larger of the shin bones, was visible, a milky white. The flesh was surprisingly pink with white patches. Her nearly empty stomach seized and threatened to return the energy bars, a bittersweet bile at the back of her throat. Then something shut down in Becca, the horror shoved to the back of her head where it could wail as it pleased. Becca dropped to a knee as she finished her inspection.

"Where's the first-aid kit?"

Eagle was bending forward to do his own inspection but the angle was awkward so he straightened it.

His eyes grew and he sighed.

After all the muttered cursing, the sigh of resignation was more evocative.

"Uncle Jim!" She waited for him to acknowledge her. When he looked away from the leg, Becca saw the shock in his eyes.

"First-aid kit?"

"I have it, Rebecca."

Becca looked at Joseph, who was shrugging out of his pack. Her father was alert—mostly—she saw, though a bit glassy-eyed. He met her eyes and a ghost of a smile, sad and pleased, gave her a small measure of courage. The smile slipped into a grimace as he looked past her to Eagle. Joseph hefted the kit and lobbed it to her when he was sure she was expecting it. She rose up and caught it smoothly. She unzipped it as she knelt down again.

"Just wrap it," said Eagle. He sounded disgusted with himself.

"What all do we have in here?" she asked, assembling gauze pads and ointment. She didn't see anything stronger than ibuprofen in the bag. There was a large elastic bandage she could use to hold everything in place.

"Just the usual stuff. Better give me the ibuprofen before this starts to hurt." He reached down and used a finger to flip the flap of meat back into the hole in his leg. His thigh muscles spasmed and he expelled a forceful breath.

She rocked back, eyebrows climbing. "It doesn't hurt?"

He looked at it.

"Not really, yet . . . but it's gonna."

Becca hesitated as she looked as well, planning on how she could patch it enough to stop the blood that still oozed. "Did you . . . have we got any more of . . . um . . . what you gave my dad?"

Eagle was shaking his head.

"Didn't think we would need that but figured it couldn't hurt to have it, just in case."

Becca opened the bottle and shook out three pills. "Enough?" she asked as she placed them into his callused hand.

He washed them down with water while Becca spread the ointment liberally along the wound. She gulped, and her stomach got queasy at the squishy movement of the fold of skin under her fingers. As carefully as she could, she worked the ointment into the jagged edges of torn flesh. Blood and dirt mixed on the pads of her fingers and when she was done with the ointment, she looked for a place to wipe the hand. Reluctantly, she used her shorts, leaving four streaks along her right hip.

The only indication that Eagle was in pain was the quicker pace of breaths and some sweat along his brow.

"Don't bother," she heard her dad say.

She looked up to see Joseph trying to remake the stretcher. Joseph looked at him uncertainly and Becca could see the conflicting emotions on his face before he resignedly set the remnants on the ground. She looked back to her task, shaking her head.

"We're going to have to walk out," Eagle said across the space to Rob. Joseph snorted.

Becca looked at the leg wound on Eagle and agreed with Joseph. She wondered how he was going to walk anywhere, much less cover another five miles of trail. Without speaking, she worked at getting the gauze on. She used three pads to cover the L-shaped injury. She glanced over her shoulder and saw a sharp tooth of rock protruding from the dirt, black on the top and glistening. She looked back and grabbed the elastic bandage.

"How tight?" she asked.

"Enough to keep it together," he replied unhelpfully.

Her lips curled down at one corner but she draped the bandage over the bottom edge of the pads and reached under Eagle's calf to retrieve the free end. She laid it over the gauze and secured it by winding the roll up his leg in a half a dozen passes over and under. The elastic tape was naturally sticky but she used medical tape top and bottom to hold it.

She looked at the rough patch job skeptically. "I don't know if it will stay up."

She heard the sound of sawing.

Joseph was hacking at another sapling, thinner than the ones he had harvested for the stretcher. She looked at the stretcher and walked to it.

"We can save the rope, just in case."

Eagle chuckled. "Starting to feel a little paranoid?"

A flash of anger flared and burned out, as quickly as it came. Becca locked eyes with Eagle. He folded his good leg under himself and rolled over with the injured leg straight. He used a small tree for support to get upright. He shuddered and winced slightly, just a crease at the corners of the eyes that didn't go away. He made it halfway and sat back down.

Becca broke away from the sight of Eagle sitting, eyebrows pinched together. She looked to Joseph, searching for help and, as clearly as frustration showed on Eagle's face, concentration showed on Joseph's.

She knew the signs, the way his forehead would crease and the eyes narrow as he calculated. Wheels inside of wheels were turning inside Joseph's head. He was done cutting and now was stripping the branches from the stick. And it was a stick, she noticed, a crutch. He had cut it about six feet in length and maybe an inch in diameter. There was a branch at the thick end of the stick that Joseph trimmed back to a stub six inches long.

To lean on . . .

He met her eyes and she saw that the machinations had stopped and he had reached his decision. His next words surprised and dismayed her.

"The fire is coming closer."

With a start, Becca looked around. She had been so concerned with clearing the trail and watching where she was going that she hadn't paid any attention to the smoke, but it was noticeably thicker.

As with the rising sun, the smoke built gradually. The feeling of sandpaper behind her eyelids seemed to be part of the new normal, along with legs that quivered, feet that ached with every step, and body parts that weren't meant to chafe, chafing. She drew in a deep breath and even that hurt along the ribs and around to each vertebra in her back. Acrid smoke sat on her tongue and her face looked as though she had sipped vinegar.

"Then we'd better get going," said Rob. The sleep had added vigor to his voice but he didn't move. He was staring at Joseph speculatively. "Unless you have another idea."

Everybody was staring at Joseph.

"I can be there in thirty-five minutes," he said, and he was probably understating his speed.

No one asked where. They all understood that he meant the truck. Safety.

"Will the radio reach the aircraft?" Joseph asked, looking directly at Eagle, then pointing his eyes skyward.

After nearly walking onto the rattlesnake, Becca had kept her head down and, as with the smoke, the buzz of the planes above had drifted into the background of her mind. Now the sound returned, separate from the rush of water, the creak of tree trunks resisting the wind. She knew the Forest Service recruited planes in its efforts both to analyze the fire and to fight it. Above, the circling aircraft had the single-engine sound of the spotter plane.

"It'll reach," acknowledged Eagle, "but I don't know if they'll be listening."

"It is an emergency. I would expect that they will be monitoring," reasoned Joseph.

"Channel one!" Becca blurted out.

Everybody looked at her and Eagle raised a single eyebrow. She continued.

"When I worked last summer with the Forest Service, that was the channel that we told people to use in an emergency. There's no real channel for it but that's the one they'll be checking."

Eagle was unconvinced but just lifted his shoulders. He looked at Joseph.

"How are your legs doing?"

Joseph laughed.

"Better than any other person here." He glanced at Becca as he softened the statement with his reasoning. "I have run fewer miles than any of you, and both you and Rob are injured. Becca has run many, many miles for a girl—"

"Hey!"

"—who is only in high school," he finished over her indignant objection. "She is very tired even though she will not admit it because she is also very stubborn. From here, she can help you both walk back while I am getting help."

He looks pretty stubborn himself, thought Becca, glaring at him while trying to figure out if she should really be mad. She wanted to be, but Joseph was right. She was tired—and stubborn!—but she also didn't like the idea of splitting up her group. It just felt like the wrong thing to do, but in the slowness of her thoughts, she couldn't articulate a good reason why not.

Rob decided the issue.

"I'd appreciate it if you'd put some effort into it insteada lollygaggin'." His words came out slightly slurred. "I don't wanna hafta carry Jim."

He looked at Eagle and smirked. Becca had a vision of her dad as a hotshot teenager, talking a bit of smack, now that he was under the relaxing influence of the drugs. She glanced at Eagle and parted her mouth to sort of apologize for her dad, but Eagle was laughing.

"Yeah, you look like you need someone to lend you a damn hand, old man. Wanna get to your feet and we'll get this comedy show on the road?"

They're both nuts, thought Becca as she watched her dad grimace as he swung his body forward over his feet, careful to protect his arm.

Joseph went to Eagle and extended a wiry arm. The other hand held the improvised crutch he had made. The coach grasped Joseph's palm and braced against it as he levered himself up on his good leg. Blood was already staining the bandage, dark against the tan color of the wrap. He tried to take a step but gasped when his right toes dug into the earth, too little muscle left intact in the shin to lift them clear.

He tried again, this time lifting his leg higher to let the whole lower leg swing free. He turned a hip and used the larger muscles there to move the foot forward before he set it down on the heel. As he moved the weight to the injured leg, he leaned heavily into the crutch.

"Doable," he said hoarsely.

Joseph looked doubtfully from one coach to the other, and then glanced at her, the concern clear in his eyes. She raised her palms as if to say, *What do you want me to do?* She knew he saw the trepidation she felt, and he hesitated. She almost asked him not to go for help, to stay with her and get the two injured men back to the truck.

What she said instead was, "Hurry."

Chapter 26

Joseph flowed away on the trail, carrying just a single water bottle he borrowed from Becca. As he slipped from sight, he accelerated to full speed. Becca's last view of him was of him straightening up to get tall, the muscles in the powerful legs propelling him at a frightening speed on trails where a single miscalculation would add him to the ranks of the wounded. She worried for him for just a second before sluggishly shifting back to her current charges.

Rob and Jim were already on their feet.

"Here," Becca said, lifting the bottom edge of Eagle's pack to take the weight while he clumsily shrugged it over his shoulders. Becca wore the backpack that Joseph had borne, and carried the remaining water bottle. Rob insisted that he could carry a pack but Becca had vetoed it, backed by Eagle.

"Let's go," she told her dad.

He met her eyes with a smirk. He was still glassy-eyed but there was an alertness, too, and an arrogance. Rob glanced over to Jim Eagle.

"Remember the first time we tackled the cliff?" he asked.

'Today, we run'?"

Rob was nodding.

"Until we die," Rob added.

Eagle shot him an amused look.

"Not today," said Eagle. "Today, we just frickin' run."

As Becca watched, both of them stood taller, feeding off the other. She felt caught in the midst of a ritual she didn't understand. It wasn't just the words. It was the attitude underneath that was masked by the banter, the utter conviction in themselves and faith in each other, the bond of men who had shared sacrifices. She watched Rob take the faltering first step toward the trail and recognized that she had made a big mistake in the way she looked at her father and Eagle.

Joseph, too, she thought.

She had taken for granted that they were like everyone else, kind of normal, because she was around them all the time. Yeah, they ran fast. So did she. It was part of the blessings that nature had bestowed on them. Now, like worn rock abraded to a smooth finish, she saw a purer essence of the men.

It was in their eyes, the way they looked at the task in front of them. Even with the theft of their speed from injuries that should have left them on the ground, the two men locked onto the task ahead without flinching. Becca found herself daunted by the courage and resilience that they possessed. For Eagle to stand on a leg that she was sure needed surgery, for her father to have survived a horrific beating in the river and a cold night in the forest took more than physical tools, perfect genetics. Despite the pain, they were moving out with little more than raw grit.

In a flash, she connected quiet strength that led her father to make the trips to places like Kenya, to Joseph. He was searching for the right people to bring back, not just great runners but great people, the ones that could make a difference. And Eagle was just like him, a great coach who worked in a smaller program that he made into a powerhouse. He didn't job-jump to the next program, working his way up the line to a major coaching job, even though he had certainly earned the opportunity. He stayed put, working where he could make the biggest difference.

Like Joseph.

She thought of Joseph and his plans to return to his country, to his village, to use his education and skills to make it a better place for the next generation. About his efforts to get his cousin out of Kenya. She wondered what kind of girl this Grace would turn out to be, but already suspected that she would like her. Her father wouldn't be bringing Grace into their home if . . .

"You coming?" asked Eagle, interrupting the thought. The dark eyes creased at the corners in amusement until he took a step, but he hid the pain by turning away. "I don't want to have to come back for you."

Becca walked over to them—she didn't have to hurry—and shifted the pack on her shoulder.

"Yes, sir," she said, and was surprised to hear an echo of the flippancy of their banter.

Her father sent an amused glance her way.

"I'll lead for a bit," he said, words still slightly slurred but clearer. "Why don' you help gimpy there?"

He stepped forward and Eagle followed, Becca bringing up the rear. The trail was mostly flat through this stretch. Eagle quickly figured out how to high-step to keep the toe from dragging and used the crutch only to help move ahead faster by avoiding putting his full weight on the damaged leg. It was ungainly, but faster than Becca expected.

She hobbled along, protecting her sore foot. Walking was almost harder than running, she decided, as the muscles in the front of her shins added to her aches. Uncle Jim swayed a bit trying to navigate over a tree root and she gripped his elbow on his free arm for support.

"Thanks," he said.

Her father would stumble occasionally but recover quickly. A trickle of blood leaked from under one of the bandages on his back but she didn't want to stop to fix it. Better to keep moving for now, she thought. She glanced at her watch. The simple act of turning her wrist over caused her shoulder to protest. She kept an eye open for a place where the men could sit to rest, a dead log or pile of rocks.

She'd poke around rocks to make sure there were no slithery surprises.

"Rest break."

Eagle glanced at her. "I can keep going," he said.

In front, her dad was nodding in agreement.

Becca looked at both of them, her dad especially. He was still wobbling and she could hear him suck in air when he twisted wrong or bumped his arm dodging tree limbs. Eagle wasn't doing any better. She could hear the strain bleeding through when he talked. He was working harder to manage a slow walk with the damaged leg than he usually did running a hard mile.

They were at a turn in the trail that led them closer to the river as it meandered, yesterday's furious flood slowed to a more normal flow. The gurgle of water against the rocks was familiar and comforting but not as comforting as the circling plane. It had been up there, watching over them—or so she imagined—while they trudged in Joseph's tracks.

Becca had made the pair of men stop and rest every fifteen minutes; this was their third stop. They argued at every stop but they were slower getting started after each one. She did a quick calculation and decided that they had covered nearly a mile. Joseph should be closing on the truck soon, she thought. If he wasn't already there. He'd been flying when he left them.

"Park it," she ordered.

Both men did.

Becca leaned against the log and took a sip of water. At the first rest break, they had tried to argue and suggested that they push through. They had ignored her and carried on the argument between themselves. Back and forth, the two men tried to blame each other for the slow progress, until Becca lost her temper and hollered at them. To her surprise, they both immediately submitted and sat on logs.

It took her a few minutes to understand that they weren't cutting each other down. It was a boy pattern. They were pumping each other up, not by telling the other how good they were, but by challenging each other to give more, and more after that.

And below the surface, what none of them would admit, even her—the thickening smoke was making them nervous.

She looked at her dad and Eagle. Neither was sweating despite the daytime mountain heat that reached down through the cloudy smoke overhanging them. The wind was gusting and brisk, tugging at her and dehydrating all of them.

"You both need to drink," she said. She coughed, her throat raw with breathing bad air.

Rob nodded but didn't move. She could see his lips moving as he talked to himself. The short distance they had covered had already started to wear him out again. A flutter of fear beat briefly in her stomach and she calmed it by taking action, getting up and walking to him.

Eagle's face was gray under his naturally dark skin, and impassive, but his eyes glowed with intense pride and confidence.

"Drink," she said.

He nodded and tracked her as she went to her father, hand reaching for the bite valve on his water system. She heard him sipping as she took a knee in front of her dad.

Where Eagle had been gray, her dad was ashen. His eyes, red-rimmed, were unfocused, and he sat very still. Every couple of seconds, his eyelids would flutter and the blue irises would dart to the side. He held his broken arm in his lap. She reached out a hand and touched him on a dirty knee.

He glanced up, eyes wide open.

"Drink."

"I'm okay," he said, reaching for the bite valve on his hydration pack. Despite the forced strength in his voice, Becca could see he was drifting back into pain. The morphine that Eagle had given him was wearing off already. Or, she thought grimly, he was tearing himself apart to keep moving, doing more damage with every step, him and Eagle both.

They didn't have a choice.

The engine note of the plane above changed, accelerating. Becca cocked an ear toward the unseen craft and it seemed as though the circling figure-eight pattern broke as the plane dropped and headed to her left. A flare of hope lit inside her. The only reason she could think that the plane would change course was because Joseph had gotten through to them, made contact.

Neither man looked up through the smoke. Their world was a trapped space of pain and smoke and urgency, a need to get back to safety before they lost the ability to move. They had no more safety nets. They were out of pain meds, the last truly healthy teammate was in a desperate race to get help, and the vast reservoir of strength they possessed was draining away with every lurching step, a cost extracted as they covered the rock and dust of the trail.

They'll be here soon, Becca thought. She blinked back tears at the thought of help. Ahead of her, Eagle was navigating around a log while her dad stood on the other side, hoarsely encouraging him. She slid in behind Eagle, ears still focused on the sound of the plane, and waited. He glanced her way. He kept his injured leg as far from the jagged end of the downed tree as possible.

Once he was clear, Becca rounded the obstruction and slipped past Eagle to catch up to her dad, who had turned forward to face the trail again. He wobbled as he struggled, but pressed on. It took only a couple of seconds for Becca to catch up to him.

He was talking to himself again, repeating the same phrase to himself.

" . . . don't . . . quit . . . don't . . . quit . . ."

Tears threatened again and Becca told herself it was because her foot hurt, everything hurt, because she was so terribly tired, but not from watching the men commit to self-inflicted suffering.

She got just behind his shoulder, the right one with the good arm, and steadied him as he stepped over the next obstacle, a medium-sized rock that normally would not warrant a second look, much less a plan for avoidance. At her touch, he stopped talking, and Becca felt like an intruder in a private world before he turned fractionally toward her, enough for her to see a bare hint of a curling of lips that was the most Rob Hawthorne could offer as a smile.

"Hey you," was all he said. It exited on a breath and he sucked another one in with a wince, and Becca wondered if he had broken ribs. The bandages on his back were darkly stained and a corner of the tape was pulling up, the exposed adhesive grayed from the particulate in the air.

She spoke in a quiet but encouraging voice. "You're doing fine, just stick with it, Dad."

Another almost imperceptible smile.

"How's . . . Jim . . . ?"

"He's okay. He's toughing it out right behind you, just like you."

"How . . . far . . . ?"

"Maybe two," she said, estimating in her head. "Joseph should be back soon."

He didn't respond but shuffled forward on a smoother stretch. Becca drifted back to Eagle.

"He's a tough mother," said the Nez Perce as he limped to her.

"He's got company."

Eagle smirked and a dim glow of sardonic humor reached his eyes. "Yeah, you're pretty tough yourself."

His comment flustered her. She covered with a shake of her head which made the neck muscles ache.

Eagle made a sound that might have been a chuckle but came out more like the sick bark of a dying seal. He followed it up with a hard, chest-clearing series of coughs.

"Crap," he said. "I think I'll skip the next couple of barbeques. The smell of everything burning is getting old."

"I haven't smelled anything for hours," Becca admitted. "I think my nose got tired and stopped working."

He grimaced as he leaned more heavily into the crutch to get around that same boulder that had given Rob difficulty. Becca glanced up to check on her dad. He moved like a zombie, shuffling forward, feet scuffling the dust and forming faint clouds from the suspended particles.

Eagle reached the smoother part of the trail and began to hurry to close the ten-yard separation between him and Rob.

"Carefully," said Becca, and Eagle nodded, focused on his feet and the crutch.

Becca broke into a stiff-jointed jog to catch Rob, feeling the complaints from her joints, especially the foot. A fast check of her watch. Time for another break. She spotted a small clearing with several large rocks that the men could use and hustled in front. She stomped her good foot around the base of the rocks and waited but no serpentine surprises awaited.

"Break," she told her dad.

He settled against a rock and his head sagged down to his chest.

"You need to eat something," she said, and fished out an energy bar. She was getting really, *really* tired of energy bars. Unbidden, a memory of a bacon cheeseburger, hot and dripping with juice, too much mayonnaise on the top bun, flashed into her mind and her mouth watered and her stomach fell into her spine with a rumble, demanding fries, extra-crispy, and a root beer. And extra bacon.

She stared at the energy bar in her hand and her stomach flopped regretfully at the sight of it. With a sigh, she tore open the wrapper and broke it in half, giving the larger piece to her dad.

She nibbled on the smaller bit, watching Eagle unwrap his own bar. He looked it over, looked at her, and shrugged before taking a bite and chewing resolutely.

None of them talked.

The sun, even through the pallor of the smoke, was hot on her shoulders. It hadn't occurred to her to pack sunscreen for a night run. She checked her dad and could see his shoulders and back reddening. They were all getting burned, she decided. It landed in the *oh, well* category of her concerns, miles behind real food and clean clothes.

She thought about dipping into the river to rinse off but it was shallow here. She'd end up with more grit on her from lying in the river than if she kept going. And wet clothing chafed. She flushed and shook her head, thinking about wet bras. The water burbled gently against the banks, clear and clean, nearly the only sound other than the noisy breathing from Eagle and Rob. Her, too, she realized.

And then another realization worried its way into her head—the sound she didn't hear.

The plane that had been circling was gone, leaving a hole in the air that she desperately wanted filled. Not that the pilot could do anything from a thousand feet up, but she missed the reassurance that help was there, close, if they did their part and got to the trailhead.

She strained and turned her head at various angles to capture even a hint of the aircraft.

Nothing.

They were alone again.

Chapter 27

Becca lost count of the rest breaks, whether it was three or four or five. Her dad and Eagle hadn't noticed the missing aircraft, but they all noticed what else was missing, and it weighed heavily on them all.

Joseph had not come back.

It was inconceivable that Joseph had abandoned them, but he had not come back, and more than the smoke, more than a missing aircraft who likely had other duties, as much as she worried about Eagle and her dad, Becca worried about Joseph most.

She tried to scan the trail as she helped the others, looking for signs that he had come this way. Occasionally, a print in deeper sand would show his progress. In the soft dust, away from the rocks, was a gouge in front of a ridge where Joseph's toes had dug in in the final push before launching his body forward again. In stretches with more than a few feet of clear space, she could see the pockmarks remaining from his passage. The runner part of her brain marveled at the distance between them, at the speed they represented.

The rest of her was too exhausted to marvel at anything. Becca's senses perceived threats all around, creating snakes from downed branches, a large stump at the edge of her vision becoming a bear or wolf. Otherwise, her head was filled with deadened cotton, so she narrowed her thoughts down to taking care of Eagle and her dad, and moving, always moving, toward the truck. Below her sluggish thoughts, though, lay worry.

Becca dimly estimated that they were probably less than two miles from the trailhead. Fifteen minutes if she could run, thirty minutes walking if they were all healthy. Now, she figured it to be an hour and a half, maybe two.

Eagle was holding up well. He grunted with every step now but was in a machinelike mode of leaning into the crutch to swing the strong leg out a stride, shifting his weight to it and lifting the bleeding leg—because it was still bleeding, Becca saw, despite the bandages—to half step, half drag it up, then swinging the crutch into position, set it, and repeat the whole process. His face stayed gray but the eyes scanned the ground and obstructions, quick and lively. He took note of the outgoing tracks from Joseph, and frowned.

Exactly, she thought, and the clarity of that singular thought surprised her.

Rob Hawthorne, the man she always considered indestructible, was falling apart. He refused to relinquish the lead and Becca let him set the pace because they would only move as fast as the least of them and their trials would end together. Instinctively, she understood that Rob was using them to push himself, pretending it was a race, a trick to keep himself moving, if the lurching shuffle qualified as moving.

Hawthorne leaned to one side, the broken left, as if he were folding over all the pain and absorbing it. Becca was sure now that ribs were cracked as bruises appeared under the bandages on his back, and something was wrong with his left leg. The motion was wrong, like he had to throw his hip to get it to pivot forward. He had stopped talking to himself, though.

Becca spied another clearing to rest at, close enough to the river to refill the water bottles. On the far side of the bare dirt opening, the trail curled away and uphill. They needed rest before tackling the slope so she signaled the break. Her dad looked confused at the open space in front of him. Becca slipped around and turned to face him, putting up a palm to catch his attention. The left side of his face was swollen with bruising and the eye was gummed shut again. The swelling was stretching the skin tight and forcing the other eye to squint. She wasn't sure that he could see her but he stopped at the hand.

"Come on, Dad," she said, touching his good arm and gently guiding him to a stump. The top was cut and weathered, a reminder of the work crews that did trail maintenance, clearing the forests of downfall that blocked passage and posed hazards to hikers. Becca tried to picture Rob clambering over a downed tree if it blocked the trail, and couldn't.

Eagle leaned a hip on the outer rings of the tree remnant next to Rob, all his weight on the good leg.

Becca waggled her fingers at him, finishing by pointing to his water bottle.

"Gimme, and I'll refill," she said.

He shrugged off the pack and stripped out the water bladder. He handed it to her and she left him with one of the handhelds. Eagle offered it to Rob first by placing it into his right hand. Hawthorne's fist closed around it and he lifted it to his mouth. He sprayed water into the right side of his mouth. Becca could see the excess dribbling from the corner of his lips.

It took only seconds to fill the large rubberized bladder through the large screw-top opening. Wearily, she trudged back up to the clearing and gave it to Eagle, collecting the handhelds to repeat the journey.

On the way back the second time, she thought she heard a sound and looked expectantly at the far side of the clearing, hoping to see Joseph. The only motion she saw was the swaying of the pines as the wind continued to stiffen. Most of the time, they were protected by the trees around the trail, but here, in the clearing, the wind whipped at them and sent small pieces of bark at their faces like missiles, stinging when they hit. Branches scraped and occasionally cracked as the air buffeted them. She stood still a moment longer against the wind, peering intently at the other side.

"He'll be back," said Eagle, reading her face as she walked, dead-legged, back into the clearing.

"No," she said, "he'd already be here. Something happened." Saying it out loud took the apprehension she felt and cemented it into bleakness.

"Lots of reasons—"

"Most of them bad," retorted Becca, then felt guilty.

Eagle didn't respond immediately. When he did, it was in a matter-of-fact voice.

"True enough," he said, "but sometimes you have to believe in the best despite everything turning to crap around you." He indicated his leg.

"We took that chance when we came looking for your dad, and so far, we're winning. We're two miles, maybe less from the truck. If Joseph is hurt between here and there, we'll find him and get him back, too. If he's not, he's probably at the truck getting ready to lead the rescue folks this way with proper equipment. Those two are the only reasons I can think of that he wouldn't be sprinting back here to help you."

"Us," corrected Becca automatically.

Next to Eagle, Rob laughed, a short sound that quickly shifted into a racking cough and he clutched at his ribs.

Becca reached to pat him on the back, almost instantly withdrew the hand, and instead swung in front of him to brace the good shoulder to keep Rob from snapping his rib cage too hard as he hacked. Mostly, she felt helpless as the less swollen side of his face scrunched in pain. She could see the top of his head, and in another momentary burst of clarity, saw the gray roots in his thinning blond hair.

"Thanks," said Rob as the spell subsided.

He struggled to stand and she lifted on the right elbow to stabilize him.

"I got lead," he said.

"Let me wipe the side of your face," said Becca. "You've got gunk in the other eye."

She efficiently cleaned the area around his right eye, leaving a clean swath in a face covered in grime. Exhaustion and pain shone but so did alertness. A smidge of her tension eased. A lingering fear she hadn't known she carried in the recesses of her mind retreated as she reassessed his mental state. He could make it, he wasn't so close to collapse that he needed to be carried.

She stepped away from him to help Eagle up, and Rob started scuffling to the far side of the clearing where the path home beckoned. He rocked in the wind as a strong gust whirled through the clearing, lifting sand particles into a clockwise-spinning dust devil. The wood smoke added solidity to the devil as it raced past them, headed east.

Eagle traced it with his eyes, and then followed Hawthorne onto the trail. Becca brought up the rear as they left the river and began climbing the hill.

It took two rest breaks to reach the top of the hill. Becca estimated it at not more than five hundred meters from the clearing and only a hundred feet of elevation gain, but it left a burn in her thighs and butt. Her breath was coming in ragged gasps and she could taste the acrid smoke from the burned pine even if she couldn't smell it. It sat bitter and tarry on her mouth. She kept wiping her tongue on her front teeth, scraping the taste buds, but it didn't help.

Eagle dripped sweat from the effort of keeping the toes of his foot from digging into the trail. He finally resorted to a sideways crabbing motion with the crutch under the downhill-facing armpit and the good leg uphill. Plant, lift, shift weight, and start all over, a foot at a time.

Rob wobbled less now that he could see out of one eye, and walked away from Eagle, doggedly forcing his way up the hill. Becca kept them together by making her dad take a longer break and giving Eagle a chance to catch up.

Smoke blew over them at the top of the hill. The plumes were thicker and hotter than at the base of the hill and, by unspoken agreement, the break at the top was cut short and they started back downhill to rejoin the river.

As she watched Rob careen down the first couple of steps on the way down, Becca tried to sprint ahead of him. A mutiny in her calves reduced her to an awkward dogtrot but she got in front.

"Focus," she whispered to her dad as she edged past.

He slowed and leaned back, making each step more deliberate, but didn't acknowledge her.

Downhill hurt more than up. She could see the spasming muscles in her thighs, flighty little twitches across the skin. They vibrated under the strain and disappeared to infect the other leg when she shifted her weight. The extra pressure on her knees ached and she resorted to a sashay; not the saucy bounce of a young girl, but a sideways sidling similar to Eagle's gait.

A bonus she discovered was that the sideways motion allowed her to keep a better eye on both men.

Eagle was replicating his efforts on the downhill and kept the strong leg uphill to balance. Rob had also turned slightly sideways to keep his good eye toward the trail. He'd taken the hint from Becca's deliberate, controlled descent, and stayed balanced.

All three, experienced trail runners, were moving cautiously. Falling uphill meant hitting the ground after a fairly short arc. Falling downhill involved a longer arc, more speed, and a much higher risk of tumbling out of control. Becca watched her foot placement carefully, only glancing back when her feet were set in well-established positions.

She wiped her tongue again and grimaced.

Ahead was another clearing. She had stopped checking her watch to time the rest breaks and started taking them whenever a good opportunity presented itself. This clearing was set on a shallow plateau with a small meadow to the side, and, as she entered it, she located a good log to sit on. The wind ratcheted up in force in the clearing.

She looked back to pass the word on to Rob and Uncle Jim when a new sound registered with her over the wind. It was faint, just at the range of her hearing. Becca's gaze shifted upward, thinking that it was the plane coming back. Even straining, she couldn't make sound come clearer, but gradually she was able to locate it.

A scattering of rocks behind her announced her dad's arrival but she kept trying to locate the sound. It was uneasily familiar. The hairs at the base of her neck started to rise and a shiver rolled down her spine.

She stared into the dense haze to the west, willing it to part and let her see, but the bank of smoke was impenetrable. Her eyes hurt with the strain as her ears identified the sound, and the little hairs on her arm rose with the ones on her neck.

Close enough to hear over the wind and aimed right at them, carried on the gusts, the fire was coming.

Chapter 28

Becca's eyes stung from the murky air as she tried to get Rob and Jim to hurry.

The initial plunging sensation that'd dropped her stomach to her groin had passed, but her whole abdomen had clenched, a response repeated by all her muscles—shoulders, arms, jaw. She had applied every ounce of willpower to initiate action, to *move*, not stand there like a doe about to get tagged with a truck bumper.

Rob and Jim plodded unsteadily.

Move, damnit! she thought, but the men were stuck at this one pace.

The trail continued downhill, angling toward the fire, but their only hope was to get to the river, and that was five hundred yards away. Both men were trying to go faster, but Eagle couldn't, and Rob stayed right next to him, no longer interested in leading the pack.

What started as a hint of sizzle barely heard over the rustling tree limbs had grown to a low roar of consuming flame, carried to them on the same thick wind that was slowly suffocating them with noxious fumes. Becca's chest burned with every breath of that heated air. Tears formed as her eyes attempted to wash out the painful residue. Squinting didn't help and neither did blinking rapidly, but Becca's eyelids continued to flutter and clean.

They hit a steep part, a hole dug in smoke, the end obscured though it couldn't be more than fifty feet away. Becca got in front, sidling down, keeping an eye on her dad. He was past exhaustion, lifting his legs leadenly. His face, the part that wasn't bashed and bruised, was listless. When he lifted his gaze toward her, up from his feet, she saw recognition of the dire state they were in, but even that was covered by a mosaic of pain.

Eagle was far more alert and angry. He pushed himself as hard as he could, testing the limits of his stability. Twice on the downhill, the tip of his crutch landed on a rock and skidded out from him, leaving him balanced precariously on the strong leg.

They bottomed out and the path dwindled into nothingness as the smoke pressed in. Becca tried to remember how far it was until they reached the river, but comparing the run in the dark to this laborious trek boggled her mind. There were no common reference points for her to measure except she knew that the river, possible safety, was *that way.*

Her sore foot kicked a rock and she stumbled as white-hot pinwheels of pain spun in front of her vision. Her skipping recovery led to a trot as cold fear rose from her gut and urged her to sprint away, to the safety of the water.

Run! an inner voice whispered.

Panting with exertion, she forced herself back to a walk. The short dash had left her thirty feet in the lead. She covered her shaking hands by grabbing at the bite valve and taking a sip of water. The rubber trembled against her teeth as she sucked a gulp of liquid, and then a second while she waited. There were no trees to the sides. She tried to remember if there was a meadow, a clearing, anything that might provide a clue. She turned to make out more details. Gray everywhere except to one side, filled with noise and a heat that beat through the filth.

She turned away as Rob joined her.

Something stung Becca on the forearm and she slapped at it, then stared. A small black particle sat at the point of the bite. Except it wasn't a bite, it was a burn, and the black speck was an expired ember. The skin around the spot was red and she wondered if it would blister. She wondered if it even mattered.

Run!

Becca drew a shuddering breath, not too deep, but still enough to send her into a paroxysm of coughing as the contaminated air irritated her lungs.

"Okay?" asked her father. He stared at her arm.

She nodded as Eagle limped to them. He jabbed the makeshift crutch into the dust, wedged it into his armpit, and took a last step to join them. A bead of dried blood lay against his side and she followed it up with her eyes to the top of the crutch. The padding that Joseph had tied to the top was stained, too.

Eagle's brows were knit together in a scowl as he reached for a water bottle to hand Rob. The other man took it slowly, carefully reaching out. Both of them drank. Eagle finished one bottle.

There was a *whooshing* roar and heat beat on the right side of her face.

Becca put a hand to her stomach, down low where it felt loose, all her nerves jangly and jumpy.

She felt her dad's gaze on her and she turned fully to face him. His shoulders slumped and he leaned toward her.

"The riber," he slurred.

She nodded and turned, waiting for them to follow. They should be able to make better time with the flatter terrain and—

She looked back and they were both standing there, Eagle staring at Rob, who was staring at her. The looseness intensified and her teeth started to chatter. She clamped her jaws tight but the muscles at the sides betrayed her with a tremor.

"Run."

Anger blossomed and Becca stormed back to face her dad.

"I'm not going without you!"

His face flashed in pain as he stood straighter and leaned in toward her again, his whole body tense.

"You need to run," he said, forcing out the words.

"No!"

Eagle broke in.

"Becca, that fire's getting close," he said. "You can get to the river in five minutes. We're going to be moving slower and we're slowing you down. You need to get going, now, while there's time."

The tears that were cleaning her eyes spilled out onto her cheeks.

"You need to come with me," she said. She understood what he said, but, every bit of it, refused to concede.

"Right behind you," said Eagle.

"Run," repeated Rob. *"Please run."*

His voice was desperate and Becca put her fist back on her stomach, the knuckles white. Another ember, driven by the gusting wind, flew past. The throaty booming of igniting wood was closing on them and the fire was like a heat gun peeling wallpaper on her skin, and she turned her back to it.

"Not without you," she pleaded. "Don't give up."

"We're not," Eagle said forcefully. "But we can't keep up with you. Now get your ass in gear and get to the river. When you get there, wade as far out as you can without doing a repeat of your pop. We'll meet you there."

They locked eyes and Becca tried to stare him down. Eagle did his best to project a stern, unforgiving image, but underlying it was a grim awareness and profound sadness. They both knew that she'd be in the river alone. She didn't dare look at her father.

"I can't leave you," she whispered, blinking.

She felt her dad tap her arm, and she glanced at him.

"Tag," he said, "you're it."

She shook her head slowly, face distraught. They hadn't played tag since she was a little girl. He'd tag her and let her catch him, and then chase her all over the yard, getting close but always letting her win. Just like he was trying to get her to win now.

Her lips crumpled together and she shook her head again.

"You haft to," he said. "Please, Becca, go."

The fire was roaring in her ears. It was so close, so close, and her legs trembled.

"We're right behind you," said Eagle, and he gave her a shove toward the river, not hard but enough to get her moving again. He swung his crutch in behind her, a signal that he would block her from returning.

She blinked back the tears, the sight of her dad and Eagle blurry, and turned to head for the river. As she did, the noise crested in front of her. Through a sudden uprush of air, the tops of the trees in front of her came into view.

Horrified, she watched as the fire leapt from treetop to treetop, crossing the trail, fed on the wind. A pinecone splintered and exploded like a grenade, sending new projectiles of ignition into the surrounding trees. She spun, to watch the path back up through the stand of trees uphill become engulfed in flames.

"*GO!*"

There was a narrow passage in the direction of the river, below the burning canopy. A shove and she was stumbling toward it. She had only taken three steps when another booming detonation dropped a burning tree across the path, a slow-motion glowing arc that lit the trees it touched before lighting the grasses on fire. When it landed, a million eager fiery sparks burst into the air like golden-red lightning bugs, and the wind drove them hard and fast into the next tier of timber.

Becca ducked her head but the flames scorched down, light dancing menacingly around her, her body displacing any shadows, the temperature shooting up, while the roar grew and grew. She felt an arm around her, followed by a second one, as both men closed around her in a vain attempt to protect her. She couldn't see now, heard her dad murmuring but couldn't make out any words, thought *I love you, too.*

The sound was worse than the heat, swelling, thrumming, threatening, but she knew that would change and she clutched at both men and thought of Joseph who had already tried to run this way, past the fire. Her father's good arm tightened on her and the roar became overwhelming, thundering down on them, and then a shadow, fleeting, crossed above them and the sound rolled back and the world sizzled and steamed, and sweet, delicious water rained down over their huddled group.

Another air tanker dropped more water on them a few minutes later, just after they climbed around the dead log. The wood was still smoldering and hot and they were careful not to touch it with bare skin. There was the buildup of the approaching aircraft, the release of water, and instant clammy steam. Through it, safe passage to the river was visible.

Halfway there, they entered an alien landscape, the backside of the fire. Blackened trees stood with wisps of smoke corkscrewing up from shrunken branches and black soot lay on the ground where short grass and small shrubs had grown. Even the rock, normally hidden from view, was scorched and black. The exposed rock radiated the soaked-up energy. Everywhere, it was hot, and the only thing not blackened was the sand, which showed bright and clean compared to the once-living forest.

They filled up on water at the riverbank, Becca sliding down to the sandy beach to ferry water back up to Rob and Jim. They drank a skinful each and Becca rinsed her face. Then they wearily trekked on. They didn't discuss options or make plans.

It took two and a half hours to cover the last bit of trail. Rob and Jim couldn't rest because the remaining logs were still hot and the boulders still retained enough of the fire to cook them.

Halfway back to the trailhead, Rob fell, not hard. More like spilling over a pile of poker chips from the middle, slipping a layer at a time until he was on the ground. He grunted on the way down and lay there, breathing hard, but he landed on the mostly intact side. It took both Becca and Eagle to get him back on his feet. Eagle did the heavy lifting with Becca anchoring him as the tendons in his arms popped and the muscles in the leg contracted to provide the force to lift Rob clear of the ground.

The trailhead was in sight the second time he fell.

This time he landed on the battered arm and ribs. He screamed, as much in frustration and fury as agony, at the injustice. When Becca got to his side, his eyes were wide. His lips curled into a snarl as he struggled up, flailing, temporarily energized. Again they braced and levered him up. He stood gasping, and coughed, a phlegmy sound with a wet, red expulsion that trickled down his chin.

Becca stared at the bloody stain for a second until Rob abruptly staggered in front. He coughed again and wiped it with the back of his right hand and stumbled away from them.

Becca scurried behind him. "You're spitting up blood."

Rob ignored her as she scampered next to him, trying to face him while keeping up. She looked back to Eagle for support but he didn't meet her eyes as he followed gamely.

She walked the next hundred yards next to him as they approached the clearing. They stopped, awed.

Sitting on the rims, the burned-out truck marked the end of the trail and the beginning of civilization, except that nature refused to concede the ground. It was hers.

The empty sockets of the headlights, plastic lenses consumed, stared at the river. All the glass had shattered in the inferno; the plastic had melted and burned clean of the truck frame. The metal, surprisingly little of the whole vehicle, was a dark sooty gray, collapsed around what remained of the axles.

All their supplies, the extra first-aid kit, the food, *the radio*—incinerated.

Rob, who hadn't looked up for two miles, stared intently at the ground.

Underfoot, a hint of green where the trail terminated into the gravel of the parking lot captured her attention. She looked down. A small weed mashed into a depression. The tips of the leaves were curled and the edges showed the signs of the fire, but the majority of this one plant had survived. As she looked more closely, she saw that it had been crushed by a foot. Faintly in the sandy grit was the tread of a running shoe, only half the foot, from the ball of the foot to the toe, with a ridge where the runner—*it had to be Joseph!*—had toed off in a sprint *into the fire.*

Into the fire.

There was another print at the edge of the gravel, chunks of rock embedded deep into the softer dirt.

Eagle caught up to her. He followed her eyes, decoding the signs for himself.

"Ah, crap," he said, with finality.

Becca's vision blurred and she wobbled. A strong arm snaked around her. Eagle didn't say anything. He just held on tight.

Rob hacked, and Becca watched as more red-flecked spittle came out.

"You need to sit," she said. Her voice cracked but she covered a sob with activity, steering her dad toward the river. The open space here had acted as a barrier to the fire. Close to the river, rocks had been placed to act as a safeguard against drivers accidentally dunking themselves. Becca gently lowered Rob onto the ground. She leaned him against one of the rocks, feeling bad that she had nothing to use as a backrest for him.

Becca cursed herself angrily. Quickly, she slipped free of the pack she carried. She filled it with more water.

"Lean forward a bit," she directed Rob, who complied. She put the pack behind him and tilted him back while draping the tube with the bite valve over his shoulder. She placed it in his mouth and he suckled some water from it greedily. The pack cushioned him against the granite.

Another eruption of coughing; a lot more red this time in Rob's spit.

Becca stared at the blood, and then looked at Eagle, parked at the next rock over. Uncle Jim was bleeding from his leg, a slow seeping. The pad on the crutch was saturated, and rivulets of crimson coursed down his side.

He met her eyes.

"We're a sight," he joked, but his voice was worn and tattered.

Becca went cold despite the summer heat as she considered their options.

"How long until they get here?" she asked.

Uncle Jim shrugged.

"Anytime," he said, but she could see him lying and figured it out herself.

The firefighters would be at the edges, trying to save the people still in the way, save homes, and livestock. Their first goal was to get the fire under control instead of chasing it. Build a perimeter to contain it, defend against outbreaks by attacking aggressively. And they were doing this for more than one fire. Unless they had combined into a giant conflagration that would stop when it ran out of things to burn or conditions changed, a wind to push it back. But until then, the hotshots were inhumanly busy.

Help might already be on the way.

It might not be sent for hours and hours.

Or tomorrow.

She locked eyes with Uncle Jim again. This time, he was the one shaking his head.

"We wait," he said as though he had climbed in her head.

She glanced at her dad.

"How long?"

The moment stretched. The question sat heavy on the air between them. She watched as Eagle struggled against acknowledging it.

She waited.

Finally, he gave a curt nod.

"He can't wait," said Eagle, shooting a fast, knowing look across the space to where Rob rested.

"I'll take it slow," she said.

"Stay."

The words came from Rob. She knelt down next to him.

"I gotta go, Dad. We need help." She didn't say "you need help" but he knew that's what she meant. "And we can't go another night out here, not without food and more clothes than we got."

"You don't haf . . . ," he started. He could barely get the words out and she strained to hear him. It took him two breaths to get it all out. ". . . to run for me."

She kissed him on the top of his head.

"I do, Daddy," she whispered. "I always have."

Chapter 29

So Becca ran.

She left the parking lot and turned toward camp. In front of her stretched the blue-gray crushed gravel of the road. On both sides of the road, the forest had burned. Wisps of smoke drifted up from the scorched branches that popped as they cooled and the heat from the wood added itself to the warmth of an unseen sun. It was uncomfortably warm now. In a few hours the sun, even if it didn't penetrate the haze, would be broiling.

Boulders, previously hidden by the undergrowth, squatted where they were embedded, black with soot and ash. The ground was the same dirty black with the occasional oasis of clean sandy soil where nothing had grown before and nothing had died. The landscape was seared and scorched for as far as she could see, and unnaturally still. She moved in a foreign world, the only thing familiar the gravel road, untouched as it wove around bends into the distance.

The pall of acrid smoke stung her exhausted eyes, but she had run out of tears to flush them. She would cry later.

It was thirty-eight miles to camp.

Becca's stomach dropped and she almost stopped then.

Thirty-eight miles.

She almost stopped but didn't, because, in her mind's eye, she could see her dad staggering into the clearing, Eagle leaning on the makeshift walking stick, both of them bleeding. The truck was a burned-out hulk and solid, rational Joseph had run into the fire and disappeared.

Becca couldn't tell if it was fear inside that was twisting her up, or the pain that was already there. Or just the pain that was coming if she kept going.

In a deep reservoir inside, a voice whispered to her. *What if you're not in time? What if you fail?*

Becca's chest locked up and breathing became hard. She compensated by forcing more air in, deep breaths that expanded her rib cage until she thought she'd burst. She forced her thoughts into line, mentally lining up the waypoints on the road, markers that she could use to chart her progress.

The gravel at the shoulder was loose so she moved to the middle of the road where trucks had packed the surface down into something resembling smoothness. She couldn't hear her feet landing hard on the road, slapping because she was too tired to keep her toes up.

What if I never tried, she thought, answering the inner voice. There was desperation in her thoughts but the whisper had no answer.

Becca slowed to a walk and took a long drink. A stab of pain flared in her shoulder as she twisted to put the bottle back. She flinched and shoved hard to seat the bottle into its pouch.

She could feel her body resisting when she restarted her run, everything going sideways. She focused on form, counting her steps in patterns of four, in time with her breathing. She was clenching her hands, so she flexed her fingers wide before curling them into a relaxed cup.

The sun beat down on her face.

Breathe in . . . one . . . two. . . . Out . . . three . . . four. . . .

The rhythm to running returned. Her normal loping stride was gone, destroyed by the miles, and the new stride wasn't smooth. She knew it, but it was forward progress. *Good enough.* She lost track of the count. She was covering ground, not fast but steadily. She crested a small rise in the road and staggered down the other side, wincing as her thighs and knees were pummeled, fighting extra force of gravity as she leaned back. The hill bottomed out and she shifted her hips to a more natural position and kept moving.

The insidious voice lurking in her head wormed its way into her thoughts.

It's never good enough, it whispered. *Still thirty-two miles to go. . . .*

She locked her eyes on the road ahead of her feet and ignored the voice. Deeper she dropped into her head. Her legs kept moving mechanically, her arms kept swinging, but the trees faded and she failed to see some of them were still green here as she cleared the edge of the burn.

Instead, she saw the Foot Locker course in San Diego, in Balboa Park. Not the first one, the regional race, but the next year, when she had qualified for Nationals as a sophomore and college coaches started taking notice. The girls were bunched heading into the big hill the first time. Becca struggled to hang with the lead pack, a dozen girls strong, but the pace was punishing. Her dad was at the top of the hill, cheering her on as her legs caught fire. She lost contact with the pack on the downhill, fading back. He kept finding her out on the course, kept urging her on.

She could hear his voice. "Hang with 'em, Becca!"

I'm trying. . . .

At Foot Locker, she had been trying to prove that she belonged, but the course beat her. The second time up the hill was agony, nothing left in the legs and her chest heaving desperately to bring in enough air. She couldn't believe how bad it hurt, her chest. She was seeing spots and it felt like everything was ready to explode a hundred meters from the end.

"Kick, Becca!" And she had, for everything she was worth.

All that pain and she lost.

Twenty-first place.

Becca stumbled and San Diego disappeared in a flash as she ran off the edge of the road in a turn. She nearly tripped into the large rocks that defined the border. She shook her head tiredly. *Got to pay attention,* she thought, and slowed to drink. She drained the last of the water from her bottle.

She could track the course of the sun in her face, the summer heat cooking the sweat off her, leaving the salt behind. She felt crusty.

She was at the bottom of the uphill now and she stopped, staring up.

Twenty-eight miles . . .

Her legs were too heavy to pick up and the hill looked so steep. She could see it turn, half a mile up, and remember the drive in, the turns as she was calling on the radio. *How many were there?* She couldn't remember. *Three, maybe? Four?* A mile and a half of hill, or even a little more.

Becca took a single step forward. Then she matched it with a limping step on the other leg. Then one more, and then she was slogging ahead again. Becca ran, head down, unable to bear looking at the distance to the top.

One, two, three, four . . .

It didn't occur to her to coordinate breaths and steps.

Halfway up the hill, the whisper murmured again in a surreal chant.

Too far . . . too hard . . . how far have you run, little girl . . . too far . . . too hard. . . .

She faltered and one leg started to cramp but competing with the voice was the image of her dad, urging her on. *"Hang with it, Becca-bear."*

The voices were getting confused in her head and she strained for her father's, heard it, and held it close. She heard his laugh again, when she told him she was going to the Olympics, but this time saw the surprised and proud glint in his eyes. Saw all the days in the sun and snow when he ran next to her. Thousands of words of advice, hundreds of hours of time. Her mom's laughter when the two of them came in, mud up to the knees because it was raining in the mountains and they had played on the trails.

Don't quit.

"I'm not, Daddy," she said, or thought she said, she couldn't tell anymore.

She ignored the signals of pain from her foot, her shoulder, the complaints of legs that were weary beyond anything she had ever imagined. Just . . . lift a knee, keep it straight . . . extend . . . absorb the impact on the ground . . . feel the foot flex . . . roll through . . . lift the other knee . . . and extend . . . and land this one, the hurt one a bit on the side of her foot, protect it so you can keep going . . . arms now, elbows in. . . .

Her feet, especially the one that had smashed into the rock, sent unrelenting messages of misery. She couldn't toe off anymore.

"Lift your knees, Becca."

So she did, like she was marching up the hill that wouldn't end. The leg cramps came back and her left one locked up briefly as the ground flattened out. Becca crested the hill and the road turned into the shade of the tall ponderosas, cooling her down after the exertion of the climb. She wobbled side to side as she lurched down the hill, back into the sun.

She used her feet, forced them to flex as much as they would. *Oh my god, how they huuurrrrtt.*

It didn't stop, the pain, it just kept growing, a little bit with every crashing step. Her chest hurt almost as much, each rib seemingly detached in pain as she sucked in air, gasping without hearing it.

The whisper tried to get inside her head again but she vaguely realized that it no longer held any power. There was only the next step and the one after that. Each step was a little farther from the voice and a little closer to the finish line. The whisper tried to tell her lies but Becca knew its secret.

Becca bore the pain, accepted it. It was truth, real, not the whisper.

She heard her father's voice again, echoing inside, reaching a deep place.

"You can do this, Becca!"

I know, Daddy. . . .

Just one step.

She could do one step. So she did, again and again.

Something at the edge of her vision blocked her path. She shambled to the side to go around. A cloud of dust made her cough. It was a rough sound and bent her in half but she took one more step, and another, and straightened as much as she was able.

A car door in the far, far distance slammed and she heard conversation, a sound disconnected from her reality of endless steps.

"*Rah-becca?*"

An arm reached around her and held her back. She struggled, leaning forward, fighting through. She tried to mouth words but the only sounds that came out were parched croaks.

"Stop, Rebecca, you can stop."

She couldn't stop, not yet, not until she reached the end. Not yet.

The croak was louder, clearer. "I have to finish."

"You already have, Rebecca, you already won. You may stop now."

Her legs were scooped out from under her. She flailed against the restraint as her face landed against hard muscle and the grit of dried sweat. She recognized the odor beneath the smell of burnt hair, this person, but she couldn't recall the name.

"They're hurt."

"We are getting them, Rebecca." The arms held her tight but the voice was tender. The voice. She knew that voice, that accent. As she recognized Joseph, she felt herself borne away. "We are getting them next." She let her head fall against Joseph's chest.

Her race was over.

Chapter 30

It was discomfort that woke Becca the second—no, third time, she remembered groggily, an ache in her abdomen, down low. The first time she woke was when they got back to camp after picking up Rob and Jim. The rocking of the vehicle as Aunt Sandi sped toward camp and warmth leaning onto Joseph in relative safety had lulled her to sleep. Events at the camp were loud and confused and she remembered clambering into an ambulance with her father while Sandi hollered and Joseph sternly directed the activity around her and the two injured coaches.

The medics had forced water into her, then food, then more water, while flashing lights in her eyes and prodding her. Someone had removed her shoes and applied a wrap to her foot. Then they forced more water on her.

The second time was at the hospital. She knew it was a hospital and supposed it was in Missoula, but she remembered them waking her and trying to take her away from her dad so she yelled at them and tried to fight. Joseph had intervened, shushing her, and the orderlies had eventually wheeled Rob away, to X-ray, and then surgery. She had nodded off waiting for him and let Joseph lead her to clean sheets. The hospital staff, with Joseph's urging, put a cot for her in the room that they would bring her father to when he left surgery.

A dream had visited with slumber, troubling her. She would call out to her dad, point to the log, as her mind played the scenes over and over. The crush of the log, the rush of the river, and the desperate dash to recover her dad. The surprise at meeting the fire, and all escape routes cut off. The flames took on faces, twisting and wicked, and her breathing would get flighty and panicked. Somewhere in the dreams was Joseph's voice and Sandi's to tell her it was all right, and she slept better after that.

Now, she heard voices again, but not Joseph's. A man's voice, weak—clearly her dad's—and a reply, a woman's voice—

"Mom!"

Becca tried to bolt upright on the cot but gasped as all her muscles seized. Calves, thighs, back, arms, everything protested, and Becca gripped the edge of the cot as the sheets fell away. She stared at her mom, sitting next to her dad, holding his good hand. Her head spun from sitting up too fast, and Becca had to take several fast breaths to make the dancing spots go away.

Her mom stood up gracefully from the plain metal hospital chair and walked around the bed with its crisp sheets to where Becca struggled to stand. Her sheets were jumbled and heaped on her knees. A breeze alerted her to the fact that she wore a hospital gown. She didn't remember putting on a gown and self-consciously tried to close the back while swinging her legs out to the floor. That's when she discovered a thick elastic bandage encasing her left foot from the toe to above the ankle. She didn't remember that, either.

Her mom got to her before she managed to extricate herself from the tangle, and sat next to Becca.

"Hey there," Angela said, and the tiredness in her voice registered on Becca even as she felt her mother's arms wrap her in a tight embrace. Becca laid her head on her mom's shoulder and hugged back.

"Not so tight, sweetie," said her mom, and Becca loosened the bear hug.

She sniffled and burrowed her head in deeper to her mother's neck as a tear leaked from the corner of her eye and left a streak along her sunburned cheek. She tried to talk but the words wouldn't come out, but more tears did, and Becca shook her head and sniffled again. Her brain, still groggy from sleep, shut down, the careening thoughts coasting to a stop, and Becca just hung on.

Angela put a comforting hand to the back of Becca's head and held her close, and started rocking gently side to side as like she used to when Becca was still a little girl.

"It's okay," she said.

Becca gradually relaxed, letting out a long sigh. The protests from abused muscles faded from active insurrections to dull complaint. A last tear dropped from her cheek unseen and her eyes dried. As she breathed in the scent in her mother's hair, the discomfort that originally had awakened her returned and she stiffened.

"Mom," Becca said quietly without pulling away from the familiar scent and comforting motion.

"Umm?" came the reply.

"I gotta go pee."

When she stepped out of the attached bathroom, the number of people in the room had doubled, and the quiet buzz of conversation lingered on the air for a second before everyone turned to face her. In addition to her parents, Uncle Jim and Aunt Sandi were there. Jim Eagle reclined in the chair that her mother had vacated, his heavily bandaged leg extended out. A proper pair of crutches leaned against the chair, too. His face had regained vitality as though the brief stint in the hospital had been enough to replenish his deep innate reserves. Only when she met his steady appraising gaze did she realize he was still in pain. It was written there, in subtly deeper creases at the corners of his eyes.

She hesitated a moment at the threshold and then walked toward her cot. She clenched the robe closed behind her, acutely aware of the gap and wishing fervently for real clothes.

Someone had elevated the bulky bed that her dad occupied. An IV rack stood to the side with a clear slim tube running to her father. Taped to his arm was the needle. Becca could not see the drip at the regulator. His entire left side was encased in white bandages and his arm was in a cast to the shoulder.

If anything, his face looked worse than it had, the bruising stark amidst all the white, multihued with hints of black, blue, green, and a sickly yellow. He could see out of both eyes though, and they followed her as she sat on the cot and wrapped the sheet around her waist.

"Well, somebody say something," said Becca, acutely conscious of the silence.

Sandi laughed and quickly sat next to her, giving her a hug.

"We were just catching up," she said. "Your dad's a little fuzzy on the details, go figure."

Becca glanced his way. Her mom was holding his hand, their wrists entwined.

"How did you know where to find us?" asked Becca. The question sounded inane in her ears but her thoughts were sluggish and she couldn't think of anything else.

Sandi paused before answering. When she did, it was slowly and in carefully measured tones. Across the room, Jim Eagle winced.

"You mean, after I figured out that you all had gone crazy and went after your dad?" she said with a glare at her husband. Eagle winced again.

Becca nodded, avoiding the subject of whose idea it was to go after her dad. She didn't want to get any of those looks. Aunt Sandi was a little scary when she was pissed.

The woman gave Becca another squeeze.

"The pilot of the spotter plane. He called it in but it took the idiots hours to tell me. I was parked in camp for news. I couldn't stand the waiting anymore so I went into the lodge and pretty much dared Greenwood to try and throw me out. One of the radio people had enough brains to ask if I knew anything about some black guy running up the road." She paused. "I figured it had to be Joseph."

Joseph's voice came from the corner behind her, startling her.

"I am not the *only* black man in Montana."

Becca partly turned to the voice. He had been behind her when she came out of the bathroom. She pictured the clenched hospital gown and blushed. God, she hoped she had it completely closed—

Becca finished turning to face him. The back of the gown opened when she twisted, and cool air flowed in. Her face stayed hot. They met eyes and he bobbed his head.

"You ran into the fire!"

"The fire ran into me," he said, without hesitation.

Joseph paused for a moment and looked to Jim.

"I am sorry about your truck, but it was on fire when I reached it."

"I thought . . ." Becca didn't finish the statement.

"I could not turn back, Rebecca. I would have run with the fire. I had to run through it to go for help."

He looked as though he were ashamed that he had not come back to them. Becca could see, buried deep, the anguish that the decision had given him.

Sandi continued. "Anyhow, the pilot said the runner was hauling ass up the road," she said, looking past Becca and pointedly at Joseph.

A sigh. "I am the *fastest* black man in Montana."

The admission surprised Becca. She had never heard Joseph boast before.

"Anyway," continued Sandi, "the guy tells me about the pilot report, I figure it has to be Joseph headed our way and Greenwood—" Her eyes rolled up, searching for patience.

"He says the runner is clear of the fire. He had put the plane back on search and said we'll get him later."

Sandi was getting angry.

"I tried to tell him that if Joseph was in the fire, you were, too," she said, bobbing her head against Becca's. "And Rob, of course." She paused. "And my husband, since he wasn't at the lodge keeping an eye on you *like he promised me*."

Eagle squirmed.

"So I screamed and hollered. He kept assuring me that they'd handle everything but he had a fire to fight."

Becca nodded. She could picture Greenwood, making the same arguments to Sandi that he had offered her. In her imagination, she saw Sandi arguing back, telling him about the rest of them. Then it dawned on her, slowly, because that's the best her brain would work, that Sandi was supposed to be in Missoula, not at the lodge.

"Why were you there?" she blurted out. Then, "I'm mean, I glad you were, just . . ."

Sandi chuckled, a sound that seemed unfamiliar in the stark room.

"Dana," she said, and waited.

The pieces didn't fit but across from her, both her dad and Eagle were nodding. Becca felt stupid and stayed silent.

Sandi smiled. "We got back into town and all the kids were acting weird, which I kinda figured as normal. I thought that Dana was just upset from everything that happened on the mountain run until she came up to me and started babbling something about sharks and bears and you."

Becca made a sharp twisting motion with her head. "Me?"

"Yeah, you," said Sandi. "Once she got halfway calmed down and was making sense, I got it. She tried to talk to you about your dad, to say sorry, but all you would talk about was a bear. She said her brother—"

"—talked about sharks," finished Becca, understanding.

"Exactly. She said you were going to find a way to hunt for your dad and wanted me to warn *Coach Eagle* to keep an eye on you."

She glared at him but this time he met her eyes with a lopsided grin.

"I did keep an eye on her."

Becca cringed, waiting for the explosion. Her mom was shaking her head in disbelief but Rob gave a short laugh, then stopped with an expression of pain.

"I think we have room on the couch," said Rob.

"You're not helping, dear," said Angela, patting his hand.

Becca peered at him. "He's on drugs."

Her dad nodded but Angela was the one that answered. "The nurse was in about a half hour before you woke up and gave him some pills."

Sandi ignored her husband and went on with her story.

"So Dana—I really like that girl!—tells me that Becca was evasive as hell and probably going to do something dumb—"

A flash of annoyance crossed Becca's face before she got it under control, but Sandi felt her stiffen.

"You had help. And it wasn't just Jim."

Silence from the corner.

"I called up to the lodge and nobody could find Jim. Or Joseph, either. It took me about a half a second to figure out that all three of you were going after Rob." She directed her gaze at Rob and tears misted her eyes.

"I was pissed and I know it was mostly because nobody told me. So I grabbed my keys and headed back. There were enough people to watch the kids, so they were all squared away. Drove like a bat out of heck but they had some roadblocks up." Here she hesitated. "The van is going to need some body work, but I got around them."

Becca felt Sandi's arm tighten around her while a grin grew on Jim's face.

"They wouldn't let me through and the shoulder wasn't real wide," she added, eyes down.

"I'm proud of ya, babe."

"Wait until you see the fines."

"We'll deal."

The room went silent and Becca saw a nurse pass by the doorway to the hall, a disapproving frown on her face. The void stretched and another question nagged at her, but she was tired.

Rob asked it for her. "You were the one that told them to send the tankers?"

Sandi shook her head. "Not me. After I got done screaming at him, they threw me out. I knew that you'd be on your way back, come hell or high water—"

Becca decided that she hated that phrase, now and forever.

"—it must have been Greenwood."

Somberly Becca considered the narrowness of their escape, her agitation at Greenwood, and how much she owed him for diverting the planes. Becca began to shake. She blinked quickly and, between blinks, Angela replaced Sandi at her side.

Her mom pulled her in and held on to her, whispering in her ear. "It's okay, baby."

Eagle struggled to his feet and rested with one crutch wedged into an armpit. He held the other one away from his body but angled it to prop himself.

"I'm gonna go lay down," he said as Sandi went over to him. "Doc says I can leave later today."

He nodded to Rob. "I'll check in before I buzz out." To Angela, he said, "Take care of him. Most of the time, he's worth the trouble."

She got up and hugged him. *"Thank you."*

Eagle gave Becca stern look. "I'll need your paperwork in by August first," he said.

Becca sat, sheet wrapped around her, uncomprehending, as he waited.

"You didn't tell her," he accused Rob, turning to face his bedridden friend.

"Tell me what?"

Then the significance of the date settled in.

National Letter of Intent period for cross-country athletes ended on the last day of the month.

"You never sent an offer," she said, and everybody could hear the hurt. She had offers from most of the Pac-12, Mountain West, and Big 12 conferences, as well as dozens of smaller schools, but Uncle Jim had never offered her a scholarship.

"I did too," he said, and now the smile was back, curling at the corner like he knew a secret.

Becca looked at her dad. *He wouldn't have held it back?* she thought, and dismissed the idea. She remembered all their conversations about schools, but going to Bridger had never entered the equation.

Rob switched from watching Jim to make contact with Becca.

"He made you an offer," he said, and coughed. "I think you were three."

"Two," corrected Angela. "Weeks."

Becca's eyes widened and she spun on her bottom to face the coach, momentarily forgetting about the gown until she felt sheet against skin. Hastily she bundled cloth around her. Before she opened her mouth, Eagle was talking.

"Here's the pitch, kiddo. All the big schools will be lucky to get you and they can give you great coaching and competition. But I've been there—so's your pop—and we know how to get you to the Olympics too, if that's what you want. If you have it in you, and I'm damn sure you do, we'll get it out. We'll build the training program to give you time to grow and get you into the bigger invitationals so you run against the best in the country."

"Olympics?"

"Yeah, quadrennial gathering, top athletes, five rings, one hell of a kick in the pants, once-in-a-lifetime shot at greatness."

Becca's shoulders drooped and her chin dropped. She'd never told Uncle Jim about the Olympics, only her dad and Joseph. And Joseph wouldn't blab. Hearing it come from Uncle Jim, the thought of going to the Olympics seemed so far away, but even as she thought that, there was an aching need to try, to step to the line and measure herself against the best in the world.

Eagle mistook her introspection for reluctance. He cheerfully pressed harder.

"Most of the big schools are in the middle of cities. No mountains there, and I can promise you that you'll miss them. You're too much like your dad that way, gutsy and chasing the peaks."

Becca lifted her face, glancing at her dad and mom. Her dad had his eyes closed but he was listening intently, a furrow showing on half his forehead. Angela met her look with lips turned up at the corner and an understanding expression.

"Your call, sweetie."

Becca took a deep breath. "Can I apply online?"

Eagle laughed. "You bet. Once you get the letter complete, we'll get things rolling on our end for the paperwork." He paused. "After that, I've got a special project for you."

Becca cocked her head to the side. "Me?"

"Yeah, you," said Eagle. "You need some teammates, and I've got a girl I want you to help me recruit."

Weariness settled in, but she nodded.

"I've got her number, I'll give it to you," he continued. "Call Dana Rodriguez and let her know you're okay."

"You're offering her a scholarship?"

"You're sleep-deprived. I'm with Sandi—I really like that girl and we always have room for good people who are okay runners. She may get a lot better, but even if she doesn't, I want her on the squad to settle the rest of you rock stars down."

Becca felt a warm buzz and nodded. "I can do that."

"Good," he said, and lifted a crutch. He turned toward the door.

"Let me help," said Angela, catching Sandi's eye. She got up and walked with them to the door.

Joseph waited until they were gone and then cleared his voice. Becca, chin still warm from resting on her mom's shoulder, glanced at him. He looked as uncomfortable as she had ever seen him.

"May I ask a favor? Please?"

She stared at him, perplexed, and dipped her chin.

"Will you watch over Grace?" Then he added, somewhat uncharacteristically hurriedly, "When you are not studying and training. She will have a hard time adjusting, much harder than I did. Montana is very different for girls than Kenya."

Becca went from muddle-headed confusion to feeling stupid. "Grace?"

Joseph stiffened and her dad picked up the conversation. "I haven't told her yet."

"Told me what?"

Joseph answered. "I checked when we returned. Her parents have released her so she will be coming soon, to stay with Jim and Sandi. They will be her guardians while she is here."

"But, I thought . . ." Her voice petered out. Becca's thoughts tumbled as she tried to process everything. She couldn't, and she gave in. "Uncle Jim?"

Joseph left the corner to stand close to her. He kept his voice low.

"It is the other reason Sandi is so angry but she cannot say it, that Jim should have left Rob because of Grace." He paused.

247

"People do not always say everything they should." He hesitated again. "I am going to get some rest," he said. He looked to Becca. "May I visit later?"

She stared at him, and nodded. He bent down and gave her a quick hug and a peck on the cheek.

"I am very happy that you are all right."

She watched him glide from the room as his words, *People do not always say everything*, echoed in her head. Her lips twitched into a hint of a smile as she realized she could hear what Joseph was saying *under* the words. And, yes, he could visit later, she thought.

The empty room suddenly felt huge. The noises of the hospital drifted into the room after Joseph, but a yawning void wider than the eight feet of space separated her from her dad.

"Hey."

Becca turned to face her dad. She opened her mouth before she had a chance to think, and discovered that she did not have anything to say, so she closed it again. The spot in her heart marked "Dad" was filled to overflowing, and empty at the same time. Somewhere in the muddle inside her were things that maybe never needed saying, except . . . except they did and she did not know how to start or explain.

Impulsively, she got up and wrapped the white sheet around her like a skirt with a long train. She walked to the side of Rob's bed and reached over the metal tube rails to tap him on the arm with her fingertips.

"You're it," she said.

It embarrassed her to watch tears form in his eyes and she swiped a hand across hers, too. His breathing was ragged, not like the strain of last night—yesterday and the night before, she remembered; it had been a whole day ago.

"I heard you, you know," he whispered. His voice was husky but clear. He drew another shuddering breath. "On the radio."

He closed his eyes but not before a glistening tear leaked out. "You don't have to run for me, ever again, and it'd be okay." His voice broke. "It was always okay."

Becca couldn't see so she laid her hand on his wrist. His skin was warm but the tube with his IV was cool.

"Is it okay if I run just for me?"

Rob opened his eyes but, this time, he was the one without the words, so he nodded.

"You told Uncle Jim, while you tried to help me get ready." Another confirming nod.

When her mom came back into the room a few minutes later, Becca was still standing there staring down at the sheets, one hand laid gently against her dad, the other clasping the sheet at her waist.

Chapter 31

On the flat-screen television, the announcers cut to the discus competition while the runners on the track warmed up for the 5,000 meters.

"Anybody see her?" asked one of the other freshmen on the team. The Bridger cross-country team, those that hadn't left for home for the summer, settled in front of the screen to watch the finals for track and field. The Olympic Trials, held in Sacramento this year and in July, were scorching hot. Times were slow in all the distance events as the heat beat on the runners.

"She's there," said Dana, as the TV cut to raucous commercials. "I don't see Coach, though."

"I don't think the coaches are allowed on the track," said one of the seniors, sparking a debate that sent everybody to their phones to try and find a definitive answer. No luck, and the debate petered out when the commercials ended.

"They're back," said Dana, and the team refocused attention on the television. The announcers talked over the images as each athlete received a cameo from the camera. A small cheer went up when they introduced Becca.

"For those of you that like long shots, keep an eye on the little runner from Bridger College, Becca Hawthorne. She's a bit of a late bloomer who's really come on this season, posting some surprisingly fast times for an athlete at such a tiny school."

The female announcer, a former track athlete herself, smoothly took over the commentary.

"She's coached by former Olympian Jim Eagle, who, in a bit of irony, beat Becca's father to lock in the last spot in the 5,000 meters for his only Olympiad. He obviously is very high on his runner and says she possesses all those intangibles that make a champion. We'll see in a few minutes if he's right."

The race started a few minutes later when the gun fired, and the women began to circle the track, twelve and a half laps to the finish line. Becca ran in the middle pack, working her way to the fifth spot as the runners sorted themselves out. The three leaders kept the pace conservative until there was a thousand meters left before beginning a smooth acceleration into the real race.

Dana watched as the leaders started to pull away and saw Becca, relying on instinct, chase them. She made up the ground to the third runner as they headed into the last lap. Becca and the other woman fought down the last straightaway. Dana watched as the first two runners sprinted through the tape. The third woman crossed the finish line four feet ahead of an exhausted Becca.

The group watching from a thousand miles away watched dejectedly as Becca took fourth place.

Becca tied her dad, thought Dana, but knew that Becca would never appreciate the irony.

Becca stood atop the towering rock outcropping, surveying the vivid red dirt of Colorado from a promontory high up the mountain. In the far distance, she could see the Arkansas River glinting in the brilliant sunlight as it proceeded leisurely to the east. Below her was a thousand feet of air and next to her stood Gracie. She had been right. She liked Gracie and they introduced themselves to others as *really* fast friends. Runner friends got the joke, others just looked at them oddly.

Jim and Rob stood behind them, crusted with the residue of sweat. The thin air of high altitude left them chalky. The girls had handled the brutal ascent better than the older men, seizing on the time on the mountain to assess each other and working as a team as they sped upward.

For Rob and Jim, it was an unsubtle reminder of age. The last time they had run up this trail, they had been invincible and had stood where the girls did, probably in the same "I own the world" posture that Becca and Gracie had. Now the trail hammered them, reminded them of their frailties, renewed the message that the mountains would endure. It had been a grunt and the girls waited up for them at the turns, until the next set of directions, before speeding off again.

Becca leaned over and said something to Gracie and was rewarded with a tinkling laugh that drifted on the air. Even now, as a junior in college, Becca was diminutive by racing standards. By most measures, she was a runner high on the elite list, but the nearly incessant testing foisted on the top runners confirmed that she would always be a step slow of reaching the pinnacle of that list. Not quite enough oxygen uptake, not quite enough fast twitch muscle, and too little muscle overall.

Becca let the wind hit her in the face and closed her eyes. She heard the murmur of the mountain and remembered its message. In three hours, they would be down off the trail. She would join Joseph, and sit with him while they watched the best runners in the world compete for Olympic gold. Now, though, in the heat of the sun with her eyes closed, she could see herself going through her prerace ritual, lining up, waiting for the gun, the speed, the pain.

Endure.

"Can you hear them?" she asked Gracie, but the other girl didn't answer.

Becca opened her eyes. The bright sunlight in the shockingly blue sky hurt but she looked into the far distance, all the way, it seemed, to a distant track.

All the tests in the world couldn't measure a champion, said Eagle to her every time they got results back, and Becca knew he spoke the truth. They missed the unmeasurable thing, the biggest part of a champion, the heart.

She looked in the direction of the host city, seeing the red oval clearly in her mind and the gun going up.

Hawthornes don't quit.

Epilogue

Four years later, Dana sat in the stands of Hayward Field, over-looking the hallowed track of the University of Oregon. Beside her was Rob Hawthorne, all his muscles tensed as he focused on the track.

As Becca took the line of her second Olympic Trials, Dana could hear him whispering a simple phrase that he repeated every few seconds. *"Just run, Becca-bear, just run."*

They were both on their feet when the gun went off and Becca swept into the first turn, tight with the lead pack. The runners jostled for position and Dana's practiced eye saw Becca defend her space against one of the taller runners, shifting her with a slight extension of her outside elbow. When they came out of the turn, Becca was running in second, a couple of paces behind the favorite.

They continued around the oval with runners jockeying in the rear spots, Becca and the leader opening a ten-meter lead on the middle of the pack, forcing the pace. On the sixth lap, two runners broke away from the pack and caught Becca. On the tenth lap, they had opened up a thirty-meter lead on her. Becca and the woman that had been leading ran patiently, not letting the other two get too much open air.

"Now, Becca, now . . ." Rob was shouting, and Dana joined in.

Six hundred meters from the finish, Becca started her kick and the favorite went with her. Relentlessly, the pair chased the leaders who, with a lap to go, were showing signs of distress. As Becca caught them, one of the ladies accelerated to the challenge while the other faded, broken.

The three runners hurtled into the final turn, separated by less than a second with Becca running third. The crowd stood and roared as the favorite swung wide of the first runner and was on its feet when Becca catapulted out of the turn in pursuit.

"That's the way you do it. . . ." Rob's voice was quiet and calm now, almost prayerful, amidst the tumult. *"Just run. . . ."*

In stride, the two women sprinted the last eighty meters. Becca caught the favorite with fifty meters left to the tape, and then lost a foot when the other woman surged again while the fans cheered them to the finish. Five meters from the line, Becca exploded in one last frantic, desperate attempt to beat the other girl.

The tape stretched around her slender frame and snapped as she finished her sprint, inches ahead of the other runner.

Becca was going to the Olympics.

Thank you

Since I own the publishing company, 10 percent of the proceeds from *Trail of Second Chances* will be donated to local high school cross-country teams.

I greatly appreciate you taking the time to read my work.
This book was written for you and other runners.
Please consider leaving a review wherever you bought the book and tell your friends about it, to help me spread the word.
Thank you for supporting my work.

Run gently, friends.
Paul Duffau

<u>Coming April 2015 by Paul Duffau</u>

The Lonesome Mile

Nick Capelletti, a world-class miler, suffers an injury that threatens his only handle on his anger—channeling that anger into running turned him into a champion. Now, a life without running stares at him. Nick does the only thing he knows how to do – double-down and go for broke.

The only person Nick truly trusts is his wife, Ashling. An Irish lass with a touch of the *fey* and a PhD in neuroscience, she talks him into coaching a group of at-risk kids in Cripple Creek–a town with glitzy casinos and gold mines and no future.

High in the Colorado mountains, chasing a pack of kids instead of Kenyans, Nick searches for a way back onto the track - and another shot at the lonesome mile.

<u>An audacious story of guts and perseverance . . .</u>

About the Author

Paul Duffau lives in Eastern Washington, along the Snake River. An avid runner, former ultramarathoner, and part-time junior high cross-country coach, Paul's running novels and stories touch on the human side of running.

Paul also has started an ambitious new project to chronicle the local cross-country and track meets in his area. You can find this at InlandXC.com. if you want to start something similar for your local teams, Paul welcomes the chance to share his experience on how to accomplish it. Visit one of his sites and send a message.

He also writes crime fiction, humorous short stories, and, with his wife, stories benefiting the animal welfare community.
For even more information, and to follow current projects and adventures, check out what he's up to at PaulDuffau.com.